C000180573

The Peak District Year

A Derbyshire Almanac

The What's on, Who's Who
and Why-on-Earth Guide
to Derbyshire and the Peak District

Paul Sullivan

CHURNET VALLEY BOOKS
1 King Street, Leek, Staffordshire. ST13 5NW 01538 399033
© Paul Sullivan and Churnet Valley Books 2004
ISBN 1 904546 15 3

All rights reserved.
Any use of this book in any form needs the permission of both author and publisher.

Printed and bound by Bath Press

WITHOUT WHOM...

I am indebted to Kirsty Cook and Marcus Milton for allowing me lengthy access to their priceless copies of *The Derbyshire Archaeological Journal* and *The Reliquary,* covering the period 1863 to 1958. My old friend and musical sparring partner Paul Wood filled in the gaps, giving me access to his collection of the Journal 1959-1993.

I would like also to thank Quentin Cooper for inspiring me to look down this particular thematic avenue in the first place. His enthusiasm and co-authorship enabled my previous book, *Maypoles, Martyrs and Mayhem* (Bloomsbury, 1994) to be published. Quentin and I have kippered together in the smokehouse of life for 25 years or more, and although we may have choked on the occasional bone, it's nothing a healing dab of parsley butter and a painfully strung-out metaphor have not solved.

The next wave of appreciation goes to Magdalena Bezdekova and Pavel Bezdek who provided the evocative line drawings. This is how Derbyshire looks when filtered through the Czech Republic.

Thanks to Mark Flett for nagging me about industrial archaeology and for adding the coda to the Magpie Mine entry. Thanks also to Emma Fairbrother and Watson Mailey for photo help.

At the cornier but no less heartfelt end of the 'Thank you' list, a mumbled word of appreciation to my partner Magda who turns a blind eye to my tunnel-visioned pursuit of writing and folk music; and to my son, Jay, who teaches me every day what a fine and wonderful thing it is to be alive.

Cover illustration: Castleton: The Garland King by Magdalena Bezdekova

BIBLIOGRAPHY

Primary sources:

The Derbyshire Archaeological Journal
(known prior to 1959 as *The Journal of the Derbyshire Archaeological
          and Natural History Society*), 1879-1994
The Reliquary, 1863-1887
Nottinghamshire and Derbyshire Notes and Queries, 1892/3, 1894, 1896, 1898
Also various leaflets and booklets from local churches, heritage sites, etc, and additional details of people and places from the internet.

Secondary sources:

Ancient Customs of Derbyshire, Crichton Porteous; Derbyshire Countryside 1976
A Peak District Calendar of Events, B.Woodall; Brian Woodall 1977
Customs of the Peak District of Derbyshire, John Merrill; JNM 1988
Derbyshire Folklore, John Merrill; JNM Publications 1988
Derbyshire Guide, ed. Robert Innes-Smith; Derbyshire Countryside
Oxford Dictionary of Saints, David Hugh Farmer; OUP 1987
Flora Britannica, Richard Mabey; Sinclair-Stevenson 1996
Ghosts and Legends of the Peak District, David Clarke; Jarrold 1991
Legends of Derbyshire, John Merrill; Dalesman 1975
Maypoles, Martyrs and Mayhem, Quentin Cooper/Paul Sullivan; Bloomsbury 1994
Peakland Chronology, Julie Bunting; J.H. Hall and Sons, 1994
Peak District: Leisure Guide; Ordnance Survey/AA, 1990
Well-Dressing in Derbyshire, Roy Christian; Derbyshire Countryside 1987

INTRODUCTION

It is said that the 19th century inventor of the safety pin got his inspiration from a Roman fibula - a pinned broach - on display at Poole's Cavern in Buxton. The artefact had recently been excavated. As a correspondent to *The Derbyshire Archaeological Journal* mused: *'The safety pin is of such wide-world utility that, if the above incident is true, it adds special interest to this noted cave. Little thought the maker of the Buxton fibula, or the Romano-British resident or visitor to the baths of Aquae who wore it, what latent goodness there was in it! Surely no other fibula of the Roman Empire has or ever will be invested with greater importance to humanity!'*

Two thousand years of history meet and mingle in that one brief eulogy. The story simply had to be told and I was determined to include it in a Derbyshire Almanac, even though I could find no date upon which to pin it. Those two impulses, somehow, sum up the content of this book.

My aim in compiling the information captured in these pages is to give a flavour of the year in all its moods and seasons, as reflected in the traditions, feasts and folklore of the county of Derbyshire and the Peak. Across this seasonal canvas I have painted vignettes of the personalities and events, earth-shattering and trivial alike, which add meat and colour to the bare bones of the year.

In 1890, writing about the role of the almanac, Sir George Sitwell declared: *'Throughout every day of its year of office it was the guide, philosopher and friend of its owner.'* In other words, an ideal book to leave by the loo. Or perhaps I should stick with Henry Kirke who, writing in his 1868 *Reliquary* article *Ancient History of Chapel en le Frith*, commented: *'He is a bold man who can afford to despise trifles.'*

P.S. This book took two years to compile, but I am aware that it merely scratches the surface. It could be written ten times over with entirely different stories and references each time, and I eagerly invite everyone to inundate me with correspondence of the *'I must object...'* and *'How could you possibly leave out...?'* kind. I can be contacted at this email address: sull@keelover.co.uk.

Paul Sullivan, 2004, Buxton

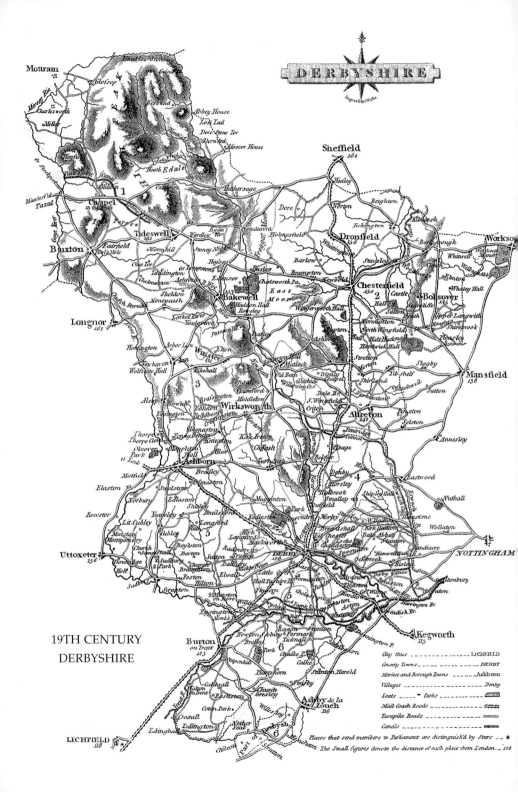

DERBYSHIRE

Engraved by J. Wilks

19TH CENTURY
DERBYSHIRE

Mottram

Glossop
Charlesworth
Mellor
Mottram
Hayfield
Chapel in the Frith
Chinley
Taxal
Buxton
Fairfield
Longnor
Tideswell
Wardlow
Sheldon
Longstone
Ashford
Monyash
Bakewell
Haddon Hall
Rowsley
Youlgreave
Alsop
Braisington
Middleton
Wirksworth
Cromford
Matlock
Ashborn
Mayfield
Elaston
Norbury
Rocester
Lit. Cubley
Uttoxeter
Dovebridge
Sudbury
Burton on Trent
Hartshorn
Ashby de la Zouch
Crossall
Lullington
Edinghall
Chilcote

Abbey House
Lost Lad
Dove Stone Tor
Derwent
Moscor House

Sheffield

Healey
Hathersage
Dore
Norton
Eckington
Holmesfield
Dronfield
Barlow
Brampton
Chatsworth Pa.
East Moor
Wingerworth Hall
Newbold
Chesterfield
Castle
Bolsover

Worksop
Whinfell
Staveley
Upper Langwith
Sharebrook
Pleasley

North Wingfield
Hardwick Hall
Stretton
Shirland
Skegby
Mansfield
Sutton
Annesley

Wirksworth
Crich
S. Wingfield
Alfreton
Selston
Eastwood
Nuthall
Wollaton
NOTTINGHAM

Derby

Kegworth

Burton on Trent

Ashby de la Zouch

City thus	LICHFIELD
County Towns	DERBY
Market and Borough Towns	Ashborn
Villages	Denby
Seats • Parks	
Mail Coach Roads	
Turnpike Roads	
Canals	

Places that send members to Parliament are distinguish'd by Stars
The Small figures denote the distance of each place from London

DERBYSHIRE CUSTOMS AND EVENTS

The includes 'traditional' events (with a pedigree of at least 100 years), plus major tourist attractions such as Buxton Festival and the various country shows..

FEBRUARY
* Jazz, Folk and Blues Festival, Buxton

SHROVE TUESDAY
* Pancake Races, Winster
* Street Football, Ashbourne

EASTER
* Flagg Races, point-to-point drag hunt
* Spotting the Mermaid, Kinder Scout
* Watching the sun dance, Castleton
* Easter Egg Hunt, Carsington Water

APRIL
* Barmote Court, Wirksworth

MAY
* Morris Dancing, Winster, Buxton and elsewhere, including dancing by Chapel Morris every Monday, various county locations
* Garland Day, Castleton
* Bamford Sheepdog Trials
* Steam Rally, Crich
* Leek Arts Festival
* Alstonefield Horse Show
* Tissington Well Dressing
* Plus well-dressings at 9 other places

JUNE
* Teapot Parade, Flash
* Morris Dancing, Wakes and Well Dressing, Tideswell
* Well-Dressing, Ashford
* Winster Wakes and well-dressing
* Double Sunset, Leek
* Summer Solstice, Arbor Low
* Dancing by Chapel Morris every Monday, various county locations
* Plus 20 other village well-dressings

JULY
* Alport Love Feast, Alport Woodlands
* Church Clipping, Burbage
* Padley Martyrs Pilgrimage
* Dancing by Chapel Morris every Monday, various county locations
* Stainsby Folk Festival
* Ashbourne Highland Gathering
* Buxton Festival and Festival Fringe
* Well Dressing and Carnival, Buxton
* Plus 31 other well-dressings

AUGUST
* Whitwell Thanksgiving
* Steam Rally, Cromford
* Gilbert and Sullivan Festival, Buxton
* Rush-bearing ceremony, Forest Chapel
* Eyam Wakes Week
* Plague Sunday Commemoration, Eyam
* Bakewell Arts Festival
* Hope Show and Sheepdog Trials
* Country Fairs/Shows at Ashover, Ashbourne, Bakewell, Froggatt and Chatsworth
* World Champion Hen Races, Bonsall
* Dovedale Sheepdog Trials
* Lyme Sheepdog Trials
* Leek and Moorlands Carnival
* Chesterfield Bank Holiday Market and Fair
* Barrel Inn Fell Race, Bretton
* Plus 9 other well-dressings

SEPTEMBER
* Church Clipping, Wirksworth
* Jenkin Chapel Harvest Festival, Saltersford
* Longshaw Sheepdog Trials
* Well dressings at Chesterfield, Longnor and Hartington
* Great Longstone Chase fell race
* Longnor Races
* Hayfield Sheepdog Trials and Country Show
* Wirksworth Arts Festival

OCTOBER
* Illuminations, Matlock Bath
* Caking Night, Dungworth
* Great Peak District Fair, Buxton
* Charter Fair, Ilkeston
* County-wide Hallowe'en events, walks and story telling

NOVEMBER
* Diwali, Derby
* Guy Fawkes Night bonfires, throughout the county
* Dovedale Dash, Thorpe

DECEMBER
* Curfew Bell, Scarliffe
* Local carols, Castleton, Hathersage, Stannington, Dungworth, Ecclesfield
* Christmas celebrations county-wide, notably Ashbourne, Bakewell, Buxton, Chesterfield, Derby, Leek and Matlock; also Christmas Lights at Castleton, Great Hucklow and elsewhere
* Matlock Bath Raft Race

TOURIST INFORMATION CENTRES

Ashbourne, 13 Market Place, (01335) 343666
Bakewell, Old Market Hall, Bridge Street, (01629) 813227
Buxton, The Crescent, (01298) 25106
Castleton, Castle Street, (01433) 620679
Chesterfield, Rykneld Square, Church Way, (01246) 345777 or 345778
Derby, Assembly Rooms, Market Place,(01332) 256201 or 255802
Edale, Fieldhead, (01433) 670207
Fairholmes, Derwent Dams, (01433) 650953
Glossop, The Gatehouse, Victoria Street, (01457) 855920
Hayfield, Old Station Yard, (01663) 46222
Holmfirth, 49 - 51 Huddersfield Road, (01484) 222444
Leek, 1 Market Place, (01538) 483741
Macclesfield, Town Hall, Market Place, (01625) 504114
Matlock, Crown Square, (01629) 583388
Matlock Bath, The Pavilion, (01629) 55082
National Forest Company, Enterprise Glade, Bath Lane, Moira, Swadlincote, (01283) 551211
New Mills, Heritage Centre, Rock Mill Lane, (01663) 746904
Ripley, Town Hall, Market Place, (01773) 841488

CASTLETON

JANUARY

1st - New Year's Day - WELL, WELL, WELL

The Cream of the Well is the first water drawn from a well after midnight on the first morning of the year. It brings a happy cocktail of health and wealth, and will bestow this good fortune on anybody who takes a sip.

For a county which prides itself on its ancient well customs, it is a little surprising that Cream of the Well observances have fallen into disuse. However, if you fancy putting the folklore to the test, the user friendly St Anne's Well in Buxton comes highly recommended; or you could take a peek in the index under 'well-dressings' to locate the county's other famous water sources.

In describing local Runesticks in 1865 (see April 14th), *The Reliquary* records that a red sky on New Year's morning is an omen of looming war. Lingering briefly with weatherlore, the first 12 days of January are said to reflect the general tone of the weather over the 12 months of the year.

In Derbyshire New Year has always been low-key. It is said that giving or receiving credit today will bring bad luck, and that no-strings-attached generosity will lead to a prosperous year. Otherwise, give or take the occasional first-footing, all is quiet.

The relative lack of folklore on this watershed date is less surprising when you consider that January 1st was not New Year's Day in England until 1782. The Feast of the Annunciation (Lady Day) on March 25th had always kicked off the year - and there is plenty of folklore attached to that date still, along with the October 31st/November 1st Celtic New Year juncture.

3rd - THE RISE AND FALL OF LEONARD WHEATCROFT

Leonard Wheatcroft, a compulsive diarist from Ashover, died on January 1st 1706, aged 79, and was buried two days later. Originally a tailor, Wheatcroft found himself on the run after his father's death, caught in the political turmoil of the times.

In his diary he records: *'Then was England betwixt King and Parliament: then was father against son, and son against father, and brother against brother. Then did I run up and down the country to save myself from being a soldier, but at last I was forced to take up arms, and was a soldier for the space of 8 or 9 years.'*

When things had calmed down a little, Wheatcroft managed to hold down the job of church clerk and Parish Registrar in Ashover. This whetted his appetite for record keeping, and he was soon making regular entries in a personal diary. He also indulged in orchard planting, building, carpentry, woodturning and virginal tuning (which sounds like a fantastic job until you realise that a virginal is a small member of the harpsichord family).

To leaven the bread of this creative activity with a bit of suffering, our man managed to get himself imprisoned for debt three times, like a character in a Dickens novel. Wheatcroft later bought property in Ashover (fleeing his 'base, cross Neighbours' of Bolsover), and his wife sold ale from the premises.

At one point in his journal Leonard mentions a visit to Martha Taylor, who was engaged in a well-documented fast. *'About Jan. 6, 1668, I and my man took in hand to go a journey to Over-Haddon to see a woman that by Relation had received no food for the space of 40 weeks. With this maid I had much discourse of God, & Jesus Christ, of herself, & of her distemper. But no food she took meat or drink for the space of many years after, as may be I shall hint of hereafter concerning her condition.'* (See June 12th for more on Martha Taylor).

The diary is full of every-day incident - an equal measure of the dull and the fascinating. This 'my family and other animals' entry describes one of his standard days out: *'I and my man went to a great bull-beating at Wensley; then to my mother-in-law's at Winster, where I had much discourse with my Relations.'* But Wheatcroft made a breakthrough in his diary technique when, in 1671, he began to compile a list of probing questions dealing with the many and varied mysteries of life. These were some of his intriguing queries: *'Why have men beards and women none? What is the cause a cat never puts her tail between her legs? What creature hath least pleasure in the world? What is the cause that a goose stoops when she goes through a high door? Why doth a dog hold up one leg when he pisseth?'*

Some of the questions were rather obscure, for example: *'What metal is the sight of the eye made of?'*, and: *'What is the cause that a 'shirm-but' or 'clock' lights most in a Cow tourt?'* The author of this almanac will happily send a case of dandelion and burdock to anyone who can answer this last one.

By 1671, at the time of his probing-question phase, Wheatcroft was comfortably settled and able to state: *'So in gardening and tailoring I spent my time.'* By 1679 he had managed to father 11 children and had umpteen grandchildren too. He nearly died in 1693 after falling down some rocks, in which incident he claims to have *'broke my head in 3 places, and broke 3 of my ribs.'* He was by this time 72, and a widower.

On July 9th 1697 our man clearly suspected the imminent arrival of G. Reaper Esq: *'I went to Matlock with*

12 staves, to get them dyed black against my burial, intending them for those who carried me to my grave.' He had planned the entire funeral, needless to say, having interred an ancient stone coffin for the event - an artefact unearthed during his work digging the site of the old church at Ashover. As planned, his corpse, in a winding sheet, was carried on those 12 staves and placed in the coffin on this day in 1706.

4th - OLD SICK, MUTUAL HEALTH - TIDESWELL

The Tideswell Humane Friendly Indefatigable Union Society, aka the Old Sick Club, was established on this day in 1764, making it the oldest such society in the Peak District area, and one of the oldest in the land (Bakewell's was founded in 1764 too).

The mutual aid, parades and feasts organised by the Friendly Societies harked back to the all-for-one, one-for-all organisation of the Medieval Guilds. The Old Sick Club was governed by a Master, two Wardens & 12 Assistants. These officials held their seats for just one year, giving all members a chance to have a direct influence on the society's organisation.

The Old Sick Club dealt with a Tideswell population of lead miners, weavers, small tenant farmers and labourers, plus a small town's usual quota of smiths, shoemakers, tailors, butchers, etc. There were also, at the time of the Society's inauguration, four innkeepers, two 'fidlers' and one 'musicioner'. These would have played at the inns and in the Musician's Gallery at the church each Sunday - before the widespread installation of church organs in the mid 19th century most churches had jobbing musicians (of the type immortalised in Thomas Hardy's *Under the Greenwood Tree*).

Tideswell also had two skinners, two saddlers, just one baker (most households baked for themselves back then), a clergyman, a 'gentleman', two masons, and one each of carpenter, clockmaker, cooper, barber, glazier, grocer, slater, tobacconist and soldier - a list which offers a clear window into the make-up of a small town in these parts in those days. (See also Christmas - Tideswell United Cow Club).

6th - Old Christmas Day - NEW BULL, OLD BULL

The wealthy Vernon family of Sudbury and Haddon Halls used to donate two specially reared and fattened bulls to the poor of Sudbury on this day. It was a Christmas Day tradition, but the Vernons, like many others, failed to observe the English shift from the Julian to the Gregorian calendar in 1752.

The Vernons had a long history of generosity and hospitality. Patriarch George Vernon, who inherited the estate at nine years old in 1517, was dubbed The King of the Peak on account of his largesse - and also because he lived in the kind of pomp and splendour normally associated with kings.

He was not averse to dispensing justice like a monarch, too. A pedlar was once murdered on the estate, and the King of the Peak summoned a group of suspects to the Hall. Each was to touch the body in turn, folk belief maintaining that if a murderer touched his victim, the corpse would bleed anew. When a certain cottager fled the Hall before he could touch the body, Vernon had him pursued. The murderer was caught and hanged at Ashford-in-the-Water, lynch-gang style, in a field known afterwards as Gallows Acre.

In a bizarre coda to this true tale, Vernon was summoned to London to answer charges of murder. However, the murder charge was brought against 'The King of the Peak', and Vernon was freed on a technicality - the fact that his real name was George Vernon.

George died without a male heir in 1567, at which point Haddon Hall passed to his daughter Dorothy. She married the Earl of Rutland, and Haddon has been the seat of the Dukes of Rutland since that time.

Plough Monday - JAG THE MEMORY - TIDESWELL

Plough Monday, Monday after the 6th, was observed in much of Derbyshire as an excuse to engage in a spot of post-Christmas alms collecting. The usual custom was to dress outlandishly and carry a plough from door to door.

Householders were invited to make financial contributions, and should they prove reluctant, the alms-collectors - known variously as Plough Jags, Jacks, Stots or Bullocks - threatened to plough up the garden or doorstep. Indeed, on January 11th 1810 the garden of one Joshua Lingard of Tideswell was given the plough treatment in revenge for the owner's meanness. However, being rotten through and through, Lingard subsequently took the matter to court and was awarded £20 damages.

Most local Plough Monday customs died out at the back end of the 19th century. The last occurrence in Tideswell was in 1901, and none of the traditions survived the cultural ravages of the First World War.

7th - St Distaff's Day - WHY IS A SAINT LIKE A CLEFT STICK...?

This is St Distaff's Day (sometimes observed on the same day as Plough Monday). Searching for a biography of St Distaff, however, will not prove fruitful. A 'distaff' is a cleft stick used for spinning flax. The word later became synonymous with all work traditionally associated with women; and then, vaguer still, came to denote the female side of a family.

St Distaff's was the day for checking all spinning and weaving equipment before returning to the tedium of the production line on the 8th, the long hangover of the Christmas season gone at last. In a region where cotton spinning became so important, the memory of Distaff might have lingered on. But it didn't.

13th - SCOTS PLAN SCOTCHED - DERBY

Mary Queen of Scots made an unscheduled stop in Derby on this day in 1585, albeit only for a single night. She was travelling between Sheffield and Tutbury as part of her on-the-road imprisonment.

Her custodian at the time, Ralph Sadler, reported the unplanned Derby interlude as follows: *'This day we remove the Queen to Derbie, and to-morrow to Tutbury, the wayes being so foule and depe, and she so lame, though in good health of bodie, that we cannot get throughe in a day - I have given strict order to the bailiffs and others of Derbie, to provyde that there be none assemblie of gazing people in the stretes, and for all quietness as much as may be done, I have written letters to [leading local personages], to be ready to attend this Quene in Derbie, with but a small trayne.'*

This was not to appeal to Mary's modesty, but to prevent sympathetic crowds gathering. The low-key approach had been a direct order from the English Queen, Elizabeth I.

Elizabeth was angered by the extra-curricular trip to Derby, and Sadler had to write to her treasurer Lord Burleigh with his excuses. *'It was full sore against my will'*, Sadler assured him, explaining that he had sent scouts ahead to see if the way to Tutbury was passable by coach and carriage. Their report had been in the negative, and nor were there any other suitable lodgings on the road. So, for a single night, Mary stayed in a house on Babington Lane in the city.

It wasn't her first Derbyshire incarceration, though - she had been kept at Chatsworth back in 1569. (See February 8th).

14th - ALL HOPE, NO CHARITY - HOPE

Charles Balguy, 1708-67, was a Derbyshire Physician who kept a detailed diary of his work and travels. As ever, the everyday details of the diarist's life succeed in bringing a past age to life.

Balguy was born in Derwent Dale (in part of the county now beneath the huge reservoirs west of Sheffield), and became one of the leading medical men of his time.

One of his most fascinating gifts to posterity was an account, delivered to the

Transactions of the Royal Society in 1734, of two dead bodies discovered in high peat moors in the parish of Hope. The couple in question had died on January 14th 1674, but it was not until May 3rd that their bodies were discovered. Bizarrely, they were then covered for another 28 years and nine months.

'Some countrymen' wrote Balguy, *'having observed the extraordinary quality of this soil in preserving dead bodies from corrupting, were curious enough to open the ground to see if these persons had been so preserved, and they found them in no way altered, the colour of their skin being fair and natural, their flesh soft as that of persons newly dead. They were afterwards exposed for a sight 20 years, though they were much changed in that time by being so often uncovered, and in 1716 their condition was as follows, viz:- The man perfect, his beard strong, and about a quarter of an inch long, the hair of his head short, his skin hard and of a tanned colour, pretty much the same as the liquor and earth they lay in. The woman by some rude people had been taken out of the ground, to which one may well impute her greater decay; one leg was off, the flesh decayed, the bone sound; on her face the upper lip and tip of her nose decayed, but no where else. Her hair was long and springy, like that of a living person. They were afterwards buried in Hope church where viewing them some time after it was found they were entirely consumed. They had lain about a yard deep in the soil or moist moss, but without any water in the place. When their stockings were drawn off, the man's legs, which had never been uncovered before, were quite fair; the flesh, when pressed with a finger, pitted a little, and the joints played freely and without the least stiffness; the other parts were much decayed. What was left of their clothes (for people had cut away the greater part as a curiosity) was firm and good. The woman had on a piece of new serge, which seemed never the worse.'*

The dispassionate tampering and prodding does little to commend the ungentle residents of 18th century Hope. At least the matter-of-fact Balguy was only doing his job.

It is worth noting that the 13th January (St Hilary's Day) is said in weatherlore to be the coldest of the year, and the 14th is said to be either the coldest or the wettest. An appropriate time for turfing up frozen mummies.

15th - INAUSPICIOUS DATE FOR THE SELLARS - EYAM

An Epitaph from Eyam churchyard reads:

'Here Li'th Ye Body of Anne Sellars, Buried by this Stone.
Who dyed on Jan.y 15 Day 1731.
Likewise Here lise dear Isaac Sellars my Husband & my Right.
Who was buried on the Same Day Come seven years 1738.
In seven years time there Comes a Change, Obsarve and Here you'll See
On that same Day come seven years my Husband's laid by Me.'

The epitaph was brought to public attention by Richard Keene in his journal *A Six Days' Ramble Over Derbyshire Hills and Dales, in the Year 1858.*

17th - COWS IN THE FREEZER -YOULGREAVE

St Vincent's Day on January 22nd, according to weatherlore, is noted for its icy weather. The parish records of Youlgreave concur with this:

'The 17th Jany. 1614'5, began a great frost with extreame snow, which continued until the 14 Feb.; & albeit the violence of the frost & snow some dayes abated, yet it continued freezing & snowing much or little until the 7 March, whereby much cattel perished, as well old as young, & in some places, divers devised snow ploughes to cleare the ground, & to fodder cattel; this snow was very dangerous to all travailers.'

Another entry tells us that the foul weather commenced a day before, and went on far beyond March 7th:

'Jan. 16 began the greatest snow which ever fell uppon the earth, within man's memorye... It fell at 10 severell tymes, & the last was the greatest, to the greate admiration & feare of all the land, for it came from the fowre parts of the world, so that all cuntryes were full, yea the South part as well as these mountaynes... So by little it wasted away, till the eight and twentyeth day of May for then all the heapes and drifts of snow were consumed, except one uppon Kinder's Scowt, which lay till Witson week & after.'

The parish records of Morley for the same year confirm it:

'March 12 - Ye great snowe broke which had continewed ffrom Ffriday seaven weekes before', and, with a postscript which confirms 1615 as one of the worst years on record, it adds: *'Note. This yeare after the greate Snowe followed a great Drought which continued the most part of Somer.'*

18th - JONES TAKES A BATH - BUXTON

16th century doctor, John Jones, was largely responsible for bringing the therapeutic springs of Buxton to public attention. On this day in 1572 he published his volume *The benefit of the auncient Bathes of Buckstones, which cureth most greevous Sicknesses, never before published*, a follow-up to his best-selling *Diall of Agues* (1566).

Jones was a very learned man, having studied at both Oxford and Cambridge, and practising at Derby, Nottingham and Louth, in addition to his favoured watering holes of Bath and Buxton. He was also the chief medical advisor to the Earls of Pembroke and Shrewsbury.

In the same year, 1572, Jones published a similar book dealing with the waters of Bath. Both these sodden volumes were reprinted as appendices to his masterwork on the manifold wonders of water, the title of which is almost as long as the contents. It can be summarised as: *A Briefe, excellent and profitable Discourse of the naturall beginning of all growing and living thinges... In the end whereof is shewed the order and composition of a most heavenly Water, for the preservation of mans lyfe.*

20th - St Agnes' Eve - LOVE'S RED HERRING

This is St Agnes' Eve, one of the best nights in the year for gazing into the future. Take some barley grains and sow them under an apple tree, chanting *'Barley, barley, I sow thee, that my true love I might see - take thy rake and follow me!'* The apparition of your future lover will then appear, armed with a rake.

For a less alarming glimpse at what love has in store, eat a salted herring before bed, and your lover-to-be will appear with a glass of water at the bedside. Alternatively, simply retire to bed without supper and gaze at the ceiling all night for a vision of future bliss, or otherwise.

24th - CAPPS OFF - STONEY MIDDLETON

The place names Capps' Barn and Capps' Close were all that remained, in the later 19th century, of the legacy of the once famous Capps family of Stoney Middleton. The last of the lineage, William Capps, died on January 24th 1703. He was renowned as a man of *'Herculean strength, superior activity, dexterity and courage; he excelled greatly as a wrestler, and invariably vanquished and overthrew all comers. In these encounters he was never known to fall or to be thrown.'* (*The Reliquary*, April 1864). He also hunted and was a fine horseman.

For all his fame in life, posterity lost interest in him after death. When a visit was made to his monument in 1864 it was discovered to be broken up, with just a fragment remaining in the exterior church wall at Stoney Middleton. Unfortunately the church nave, Capps' original resting place, had been dismantled in 1758.

25th - The Feast of St Paul's Conversion - HERE COMES THE SUN

St Paul's symbol on local Runesticks (see April 14th) was often the Sun, a reference to weatherlore which maintains that any sunshine at all today, *'even so long only as it takes to mount a horse'*, indicates a good year. The rest of the day's lore insists that storms presage war, fog brings sickness, and snow and rain mean famine.

War can sometimes be pre-empted from the most unlikely sources. The singing of Stormcocks (mistle thrushes) from tall trees or buildings in January is a portent of tempests. As noted above, storms themselves indicate war. This thrush-lore is something of an irony, given that another country name for the bird is January Joy, a title more in tune with the old saying that a mistle thrush singing at sunset heralds a fine day ahead.

30th - PARDON ME WHILE I DECAPITATE YOU - CHARLES I

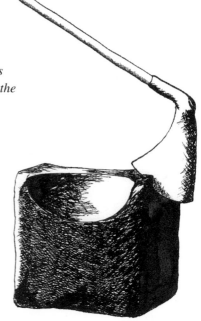

The death of King Charles I on this day in 1649 was described in a piece of on the spot reportage by Robert Cochet of Mickleover (1611-57). Cochet called himself *'an eye witness of the highest action which was ever acted on the English stage'*.

He mentions how the King appeared at 2pm, approaching the block and axe *'at which he smilingly looking found fault with the block for being made too lowe.'* Fourteen others were crowding the scaffold with Charles. He chatted to these for a quarter of an hour - and what a surreal few minutes those must have been for all concerned. Then, *'the executioner having on his knees asked him pardon cutt off his head at one blow and his mate tooke it upp and held it upp to the spectators which was very many. The executioners were disguised being masqued with great beards and I believe not known to many. The king seemed to die resolutely... There was much scrabbling for the kings blood.'*

The event receives far more brevity in the commemorative inscription in the Church of All Saints, Brailsford: *'CR began his R 1625, March 27th: set up his standard at Nottingham, 22nd August 1642. Beheaded at Whitehall 1649, January 30th'.*

But then the church here has every cause to be eccentric - Brailsford was recorded in the Domesday Book of 1086 as having just half a church, as it straddled a parish boundary.

30th - HARD CAW - BOYLESTON

Enlightened 17th century Derby physician, Percival Willoughby, showed a chink in his rationalist armour on January 30th 1672. He noted in his journal that a case he had attended at Boyleston was complicated by the patient's convulsions. Willoughby took the cawing of rooks outside as an ill omen. Sure enough, his patient died, he received no pay for his ill-fated administrations, and he declared himself relieved to get back home.

Hardly a glowing advert for the man's skills. This is a busy time for rooks, of course, with nest building and other noisy preparations for the mating season. It would be very hard *not* to hear them at this time of year.

30th - WHO'S THE DAFTEST AFTER ALL? - CASTLETON

Sammy Eyre, aka Daft Sammy, Soft Sammy or Sammy Scut, was born in Castleton in 1806. He became a lead miner in his teens; but his knowledge of the village and its multiple delights was so detailed and enthusiastic that he also pursued a career as unofficial tour guide, and was soon able to abandon the mines altogether.

He charged no fee for his tours and local information, but was nearly always given financial reward for his efforts - he would, of course, emphasise to any new party how generous the previous lot had been.

His specialities included helping people up the steep road under Mam Tor (closed since its collapse in 1976), and carrying women across streams. His trademark patchwork coat was said to have been ripped by the legions of fearful hands hanging onto him during the ascent of Mam Tor.

Richard Keene in his journal, *A Six Days' Ramble Over Derbyshire Hills and Dales in the Year 1858*, suggests that Sammy wasn't up to all tasks:

'Before reaching the Speedwell Cavern, we came across Soft Sammy - or more correctly speaking, he came across us, for it is his business to waylay all strangers - but he was not soft enough to help to pull our cart up the Winnats, not he; however, as he was not willing to work, he got no pay, and soon left us. Hercules! What a pull it was up that steep and stony road.'

Sammy grew old before his time, and in these later years he was often reduced to charging an unofficial admission fee from his seat beneath Peveril Castle. He died in the Chapel-en-le-Frith workhouse on this day in 1868. The Castleton villagers, who had fed and sheltered the man over the years, held a concert to raise money to erect a tombstone - a touching conclusion to an eccentric life.

These days, of course, all the extortion and begging that Sammy Eyre carried out is overseen by various official bodies as part of Castleton's formidable tourist industry. He was more entrepreneur than beggar, and the 'daft' tag hardly seems fair. But that's posterity for you.

ALL SAINTS, BAKEWELL

FEBRUARY

1st - St. Bride's Day - ALMOST SERPENTLY NOT - ARBOR LOW

In that confusing and confused melting pot where the Early Church meets its pagan predecessors, St Bride looms large. Christianity appears to have inherited large chunks of the legends of the Celtic goddess Bride (pronounced Breed-a) and grafted them onto the life of St Brigid of Ireland (whose feast day it is today).

Part of the folklore equates Bride with snakes. At Glenelg in Scotland she is even said to appear on this day as a gigantic Serpent Queen. The tenuous link to Derbyshire is this: Thomas Bateman, a renowned Derbyshire antiquary, published an account of Arbor Low in 1848 (*Vestiges of the Antiquities of Derbyshire*), in which he made claims that the site had once been associated with serpent-worship:

'About a quarter of a mile from Arbor Low in a westerly direction, is a large conical tumulus known as Gib Hill, which is connected with the vallum of the temple by a rampire of earth, running in a serpentine direction, not dissimilar to the avenue through the celebrated temple of Abury [Avebury]. *To any believer in the serpent worship of the Celtic tribes this fact will be of interest.'*

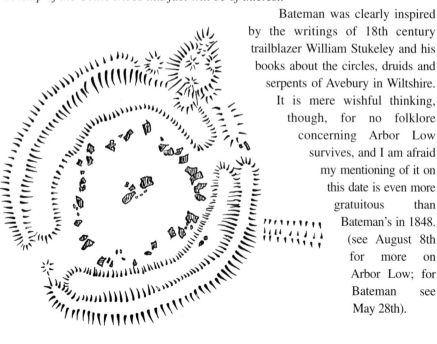

Bateman was clearly inspired by the writings of 18th century trailblazer William Stukeley and his books about the circles, druids and serpents of Avebury in Wiltshire. It is mere wishful thinking, though, for no folklore concerning Arbor Low survives, and I am afraid my mentioning of it on this date is even more gratuitous than Bateman's in 1848. (see August 8th for more on Arbor Low; for Bateman see May 28th).

2nd - POEM A-PEAL - BAKEWELL

Bakewell received new bells on this day in 1797, and they were rung-in by some celebrated campanologists from Sheffield. They were paid for by subscription - the Dukes of Devonshire and Rutland chipped in, along with a couple of reverends and a huge host of social 'wannabees'. Inscribed on the bells were many whimsical and philosophical couplets, including:

> *Mankind like us too oft are found*
> *Possessed of nought but empty sound.*

> *When of departed hours we toll the knell*
> *Instruction take and spend the future well.*

> *When men in Hymens bands unite*
> *Our merry peals produce delight*

> *But when death goes his dreary rounds*
> *We send forth sad and solemn sounds.*

> *Would men like us join and agree*
> *They'd live in tuneful harmony.*

2nd - Candlemas Day - WATCH THE WIND

This is Candlemas Day, and local weatherlore maintains: *When the wind's in the East on Candlemas Day, there it'll bide till the end of May.*

Furthermore, you are advised that: *Candlemas day, put beans in the clay, but candles and candlesticks all away.*

This is also the traditional date for the appearance of snowdrops, which are known as February Fair Maids or Candlemas Bells. Girls would sometimes wear the flowers at Candlemas as a symbol of purity.

3rd - St Blaise's Day - ANOTHER BLAISE OF WIND

St Blaise's Day comes at you with yet more weatherlore. According to local wisdom, windy weather today is a portent of a windy year.

MUST HAVE BEEN ALL
YESTERDAY'S BEANS.

There's no let up from the bad weather over the coming days, I'm afraid. On the feast of St Dorothea, February 6th, it is said *Dorothea gives the most snow.*

5th - SUNDAY MASS MURDER - CHURCH PEST CONTROL

On this day in 1748, Stephen Broomhead, the Dog Whipper of Eyam, died. It had been his job to enter the church every Sunday morning and evict the canine squatters with his ash and leather whip.

He was not mauled to death by an irate cur, but was dogged by bad weather: *'...overlaid in y snow upon Eyam Moor'*, according to his death entry in the registers.

Broomhead was not alone in his vocation. Other practitioners include these two from the parish records of Hartshorn:

1787.   William Heaton for Whiping the Dogs, 5 shillings

1804.   Paid William Rose for shoes for Robert Jaques for putting dogs out of the church &c 10 shillings

These same records have a number of entries for killing badgers (worth a shilling), and reveal that in 1746 a dozen sparrows *'such as appear in full feather with the Bodies'* brought the hunter 2d a bunch.

Evidence of sparrow shooting has been found during many Derbyshire church restorations in the form of lead shot embedded in the interior timbers, acting as a strange historical receipt for each of those tuppenny bunches.

Another dogged record from Chapel-en-le-Frith reads:

1755.   Paid George Bramwell for wiping doggs and walking in church on Sundays. 10 shillings.

These records also record handsome payments for foxes (11 shillings), and between one and two shillings for badgers, hedgehogs and ravens' heads.

5th - A GOOD DAY TO DIE - PARISH RECORDS

The various county parish records report a number of deaths on this day, in very different circumstances. The first befell proto-aristocrat William Peverell, who died in 1113. From the first flush of Norman land-grabbers following the Conquest in 1066, the Peverells had charge of the Manor of Hope, a large chunk of the Derbyshire High Peak, and William is recorded as holding such in Domesday (1086). The Manor included Tideswell, Hope, Castleton and Bradwell, amongst others.

The Darley Dale registers report an early mining casualty, with one Roger Ball killed *'in a grove'* (a local word for mine) on this day in 1676.

Monyash parish records note the deaths on February 5th 1772, of *'John Allcock, blacksmith, and Richard Botham, a baker. N.B. These two were starved to death coming from Winster market, on Middleton Common.'* Another grim reflection of the realities of poor communications and terrible weather.

7th - O FORTUNATUS! - DARLEY DALE

This was the birth day of Henslow Fotherley Fortunatus Williamson in 1698, according to the Darley Dale registers. Henslow was witness to the fact that daft names were not something invented by hippies in the 1960s.

As a further example from the same records there is a reference on April 24th 1671 to the wedding of Mrs Mary Potte to Mr ffrancis ffolmbige-bache. Again, there was a marriage on January 9th 1615 which produced Mrs Wallbrydge Collombell; and on February 2nd 1642 a blushing bride took the wonderful name of Bersheba Wildgoose.

8th - MARY, PILLAR OF THE COMMUNITY - POOLE'S CAVERN

This was the day on which Mary Queen of Scots was executed at Fotheringhay, Northamptonshire, in 1587. Mary had stayed occasionally in Derbyshire during her years as Elizabeth I's prisoner, including a stint at Chatsworth, a night in Derby (see Jan 13th), and a brief stay early in the 1580s in the country lodge of the Earl of Shrewsbury, in what is now The Old Hall Hotel, Buxton.

During this time she is reputed to have visited Buxton's famous show cave, Poole's Cavern. Legend says that, although suffering badly with rheumatism, Mary braved the cave's damp and cramped subterranean spaces and travelled by candlelight to the feature now known as the Queen of Scots Pillar - needless to say, named in her honour. Before a further chamber was opened up in the 19th century this was as far as you could walk in the Cavern. It was also much harder to gain access in the first place - blasting and digging have since made things easier for tourists.

13th - BESS RAISES HER GLASS - HARDWICK HALL

On this day in 1608 the famed Elizabeth 'Bess of' Hardwick died, aged 87. She is known as the Matriarch of Derbyshire Gentry, having had four husbands and given birth to the first Duke of Devonshire.

Owning much of the region's land and money, Bess was responsible for many of its finest buildings, including Chatsworth and Hardwick Hall. The latter was celebrated at the time for its

HARDWICK OLD HALL

ingenious construction, recorded in the local rhyme:

'Hardwick Hall, more glass than wall!'

Self-appointed Peak poet laureate, Charles Cotton, described the first Chatsworth, built in 1572 for £60,000, as *'a stately and stupendous pile'*. Very little remains of this, however - what you see today was commenced by the 4th Duke of Devonshire in the 1690s. (See February 17th for Cotton).

13th-14th - Valentine's Eve and Day -

Valentine's Eve and the following morning were reckoned a good time for divination on the question of love. In Derbyshire one of the favourite methods was for girls to gather hemp and run round the church chanting something along the lines of:

Hempseed I sow, hempseed I sow,
He that loves me best come after me and mow!

Their future partners would then appear before them in a haze of hempseed magic. Don't try this at home, at least not until the use of certain herbs is legalised.

Alternatively, you can look through the keyhole of a hen house. If a cock and hen are side by side, you will be married before the end of the year.

William Newton, the 'Minstrel of the Peak', wrote on February 14th 1795:

To My Wife, On Valentine's day.

And shall this day, which brings such joy
To every vagrant Girl and Boy,
Which brings to toying little Misses
Such reams of paper, gloves and kisses,
Shall such a day to Mirth devoted
Pass by me dully and unnoted?

Sadly not.... but, mercifully, the editorial hand can spare you the gory details. (See November 3rd for more on Newton).

In the High Peak area any girl not kissed, visited or greeted in some way by a man on this day was called 'Dusty'. Her punishment for this was a dose of Sweeping. This involved the unfortunate one being abused with a broom or bunch of straw. After this indignity the luckless girl had the option of entering a lottery to find out who her lover would be - names were put in a hat, and the girls would try a spot of lucky dip.

A general rule maintains that the first person you meet on Valentine's morning will be your lover for the rest of the year. Family and animals don't count, but there is nothing in the folklore stipulating the sex of the person - so beware.

15th - ALL NOTE, NO QUERY

The Nottinghamshire and Derbyshire Notes and Queries is a repository of historical, archaeological and general local information that books like mine plunder mercilessly for their material. It therefore comes as a surprise to learn that *Notes and Queries* struggled from the onset, lacking in sponsors and bemoaning the lack of input from the Derbyshire side of the equation. It nearly foundered after the first volume (1892/3), and the final edition of that year had a desperate article entitled *To Be Or Not To Be?*

It was only by reaching deeply into their own pockets that the prime movers were able to continue the enterprise. When volume 2 hobbled off the presses, the editor grabbed the nearest nautical metaphors and bludgeoned his apathetic audience:

In commencing our second volume, we desire to point out that it is more owing to our perseverance than to any access of support that we are venturing on a second voyage in our frail barque. We have practically suffered shipwreck, but, even with one officer [the assistant editor, who had been headhunted by the museum in Cardiff] *overboard (and but an inexperienced one in his place), we are once more tempting the winds and waves of fortune. If we succeed in bringing our ship to port we shall believe that, like Sempronius, we have 'deserved success'.*

Sadly, *Notes and Queries* managed only a short voyage. But what it bequeaths to us is priceless.

17th - FISHING WITH COTTON - THE WONDERS OF THE PEAK

Champion of anything to do with fishing and Derbyshire - notably Dovedale - author Charles Cotton died on this day in 1687. He was born, and lived most of his life, in the now ruined Hall in Beresford Dale.

These days Cotton is famous for his part in that perennial best-seller *The Compleat Angler*, written by Izaac Walton. Cotton provided a section on fishing in

Derbyshire, which appeared in the fifth edition, 23 years after the first, in 1676. Cotton's connection with the River Dove is commemorated in the Charles Cotton Hotel in Hartington, where residents can get permits for fly fishing (as with many of the hotels in the vicinity of the Dove).

For tourists of earlier ages, Cotton was probably best known, not as an angler, but as the author of the book *Wonders of the Peak* (1681), which took its cue from the earlier work by Thomas Hobbes, *De Mirabilibus Pecci: Concerning the Wonders of the Peak in Darby-shire* (1636). Cotton describes the 'Seven Wonders' in melodramatic verse:

> *...They call them Wonders there, and be they so,*
> *But the whole Country sure a wonder too.*

One of them is Peak Cavern in Castleton: *...a dreadful cave, Whose light may well astonish the most brave.* Another is Eldon Hole, reckoned in folklore to be bottomless or, at the very least, marvellously deep:

> *...And he, that standing on the brink of Hell,*
> *Can carry it so unconcerned, and well,*
> *As to betray no Fear, is certainly*
> *A better Christian: or a worse than I.*

The other candidates are the 'stupendous pile' of Chatsworth (the foremost Wonder, according to Cotton); St Anne's Well and Poole's Cavern in Buxton; Mam Tor near Castleton; and the obscure Ebbing and Flowing Well in Tideswell (which stopped ebbing and flowing in 1790 after the installation of a new water pipe system).

Only the most cynical would concur with sour-faced critic Henry Kirke who, in 1903, wrote witheringly on the subject of the Seven Wonders: *'Buxton Well is but one amongst a score of similar springs in England, Mam Tor is an inconsiderable hill of loose shale, Eldon Hole a small chasm in the mountain limestone, and the Ebbing and Flowing Well a mere row of befouled cattle troughs.'*

After the restoration of Charles II, Charles Cotton worked as revenue commissionaire for Derbyshire and Staffordshire. This was something of an irony given that he had been in the habit of amassing huge debts and then hiding from his creditors in caves in Beresford Dale. Indeed, debt forced him to sell Beresford Hall to his cousin, John Beresford, in 1681, although Cotton lived on at the Hall until his death. He is buried at St James', Piccadilly, in London.

18th - MASS PROTEST - ALFRETON

On February 1635, Thomas Brooke, Vicar of Alfreton, was brought before the church authorities, who for several years had been unhappy with the man's increasing non-conformity. The main complaint against him was that he had recently cancelled Sunday Communion.

It appears that after arguing with men sent to erect a rail around the communion table, Brooke, on the first Sunday in the year, *'absented himself and caused the church doors to be locked up so that there was not any communion at all, nor divine service that day in the forenoon.'* Brooke was excommunicated for his troubles.

22nd - THE WEATHER FORECAST FOR THE NEXT FORTY DAYS

Weatherlore tries to persuade us that this is the first day of Spring, and whatever the conditions today, there will be no significant change in the weather for the next 40 days.

24th - KING'S EVIL TOUCH NO GOOD - CURES FOR SCROFULA

David Wheatcroft was the third eldest son of Derbyshire diarist Leonard Wheatcroft (see January 3rd). On this day in 1686 David went to visit James II, *'to be touched by him for his infirmity called the King's Evil. There was he touched twice by him, but was never the better at his retourne'.*

James was the last king to attempt the hands-on 'cure' for scrofula, the so-called King's Evil. His sister Queen Anne was the last to try it. As part of the King's Evil ceremony the monarch would read from Mark xvi 14, culminating with *'They shall lay hands on the sick and they shall recover.'* This was followed by a reading from John i1, after which a gold coin in a bag was placed around the sufferer's throat. There were more prayers, and that was that.

One Oxford man, who took the cure as a youngster in Anne's reign, demurred when asked if the cure worked, saying he had no 'Evil' about him in the first place, and that his poor parents had *'no objection to the bit of gold'*, which may be a clue as to why the tradition had survived so long.

David, after his failure at the King's hands, next tried an approach which had supposedly cured his scrofulous aunt Sarah, a resident of Shottle. His father describes the cure like this: *'That a man might go to a dead woman or a woman to a dead man and with their dead hand touch all their affected or sore places, saying these words "he that send thee, I pray God mend thee." That must be done, and said nine times over - which David did Dec 26, 1687.'*

Alternatively, a fasting virgin could lay her hands on the sores, say certain words, and then spit on the wounds three times. Sadly it was all to no avail, and David died on October 15th 1688, aged 20.

24th - St Matthias's Day - TO BEE OR NOT TO BEE

Bees beware. This is St Matthias's Day, when apiarists are supposed to 'shut up the bee' in hives. The importance of this is backed up by a rhyme which insists:

> *If bees get out in February,*
> *The next day will be rough and rainy.*

27th - TALL TALES -
LITTLE JOHN IN HATHERSAGE

Leonard Wheatcroft visited the grave of Little John on this day in 1685: *'I went to hather'seige where we beheld the grave where they say Little John was buried, which is 14 foot in length.'*

This is one of the earliest references to the local landmark in Hathersage churchyard, which, if you believe the legends, is indeed the resting place of Robin Hood's sidekick. He is said to have ended his life in a cottage which used to stand to the east of the churchyard - something referred to in this quote from the less-than-impressed Richard Keene, writing in 1858:

'Little John's Grave was rather a disappointment in a photographic point of view, as it consisted only of two very small stones at a very great distance apart... At a short distance to the south-east of the church is the ancient cottage where he came to die - Jenny Sheard's cottage. We found the cottage, but Jenny Sheard was dead; her nephew, however, lived in it, an old man, and on asking him whether this really was the cottage in which Little John died, he replied 'Ay, I reckon this is it'.'

A huge longbow, some chain mail and a green cap, all said to belong to Little John, were decorating the church as late as the mid-18th century. They were removed due to the poor state of the church roof, which was letting in so much water that there were weeds growing in the aisle. After their removal the legend was given a further boost when an examination of the grave in 1784 unearthed a huge human thigh bone, nearly a metre long. Little John or no Little John, the grave is now tended by the Ancient Order of Foresters Friendly Society, which seems a very appropriate custodianship.

28th - ALL IS FINE WITH THE BELL-RINGERS - HATHERSAGE

At Hathersage's rectory a ghostly woman in white is alleged to appear this evening. She opens one of the doors, and then skips back to the Other Side. None of which is directly related to the following lines written in 1650 as a record of the Hathersage bell-ringers' system of tongue in cheek fines. The fines paid for the ringers' annual feast (see November 5th):

You gentlemen that here with to ring
See that these laws you keep in everything,
Or else be sure you must without delay
The penalty thereof to the ringers pay.

First when you into the bellhouse come
Look if the ringers have convenient room
For if you be a hindrance unto them
Fourpence you forfeit unto these gentlemen.

Next if you here do intend to ring
With hat or spur, do not touch a string
For if you do your forfeit is for that
Just fourpence down to pay, or lose your hat.

If you a bell turn over, without delay
Fourpence unto the ringers you must pay,
Or if you strike, miscall or do abuse
You must pay fourpence for the ringers' use.

For every oath here sworn, ere you go hence
Unto the poor you must pay twelvepence;
And if that you desire to be enrolled
A ringer here, these orders keep and hold.

But whoso doth these orders disobey
Unto the stocks we will take him straightway
There to remain until he is willing
To pay his forfeit and the clerk a shilling.

29th - LEAP OF FAITH

It is said that anyone born on this auspicious once-in-every-four-years day will be pursued by good fortune throughout their lifetime.

Apocryphal Biblical lore maintains that this was the birthday of Job, whose famous patience was divinely translated into good fortune. The downside is that in

Leap Years broad beans never prosper, and sheep tend to pine.

The 29th itself is the best day for a woman to propose to a man, but only if she is wearing red petticoats - something of a dilemma in these days of hipsters and crop tops.

SHROVETIDE TRADITIONS

Shrovetide covers the Monday and Tuesday before the forty days of Lent - a time of pancakes and much else besides.

COLLOP MONDAY - BRINGING HOME THE BACON

This, the Monday before Shrove Tuesday, is named after the traditional dish of the day: collops of bacon served with eggs. The poor of the region would beg the meat from their richer neighbours. In addition to providing a little meat, the collops were also the source of the fat for the following day's pancakes.

Collop Monday was observed as a Mischief Night in some areas, including Great Longstone. Children here would pinch items such as gates, furniture and garden implements and pile them around the village cross for the owners to rummage through in the morning.

PANCAKES - OUT OF THE FRYING PAN INTO THE MIDDEN

Winster stages its Pancake Race every Shrove Tuesday - a strange cross between *Ready, Steady, Cook* and a school sports day. Children spend the morning mixing the special 'race batter', but they don't bother saving a portion for tea time - these particular pancakes are not meant to be edible, but are thick and durable in order to withstand vigorous tossing. The small, light frying pans used in the event are known as 'racing pans'.

Competitors gather mid-afternoon outside the town's ancient Market House, and there are separate events for children, women and men, along a course known as The Gallops. During the race the pancakes must be flipped at least three times, and if the thing flops to the ground you have to stop and put it back in the pan. The fastest tosser in town is the winner. The Winster Morris Men have a tune which commemorates the event, *The Winster Gallop*, a very catchy little polka.

Back with the edible variety, in days long gone Whaley Bridge girls faced a Shrove Tuesday pancake eating challenge. The girl's mother would make the delicacy, and the reluctant participant had to consume it before a second one was cooked. The penance for failure varied, but included the threat of being thrown into a gooseberry bush or an ash pit (the euphemism for an outdoor midden, or latrine).

PANCAKE BELLS - ONE BARRED CHURN DESERVES ANOTHER

In most villages the Pancake Bell was rung at 11am on Shrove Tuesday, marking a holiday for the children. At Ashford-in-the-Water the treats, sweets and general fun, led to the day being known as Goody's Tuesday.

At Dronfield the children had to listen to the pealing bell for half an hour before being released from the classroom. The custom here was to go to the church with a large basket in the wholly unsubstantiated belief that pancakes would be thrown over the church roof for the children to collect.

The Pancake Bell was, indeed, originally a call to church, and a symbolic end to the curfew bells of the winter season. Some parishes still peal the bells on Shrove Tuesday, in accordance with the ancient tradition.

As part of the one-day holiday proceedings, Barring Out was a popular escapade for the region's schoolchildren, including those at Tideswell, Great Hucklow and Eyam. Pupils would bar the door on their teachers until they had been granted the half-day break promised by the Pancake Bell, chanting a verse along the lines of:

> *Bar, master, bar, bar for a pin,*
> *If you won't give us a holiday we won't let you in.*

The outcome varied in the latter days of the tradition. In the early 20th century children would sometimes be granted the time off, but more often than not they were simply punished for having the audacity to invoke an ancient tradition. Little wonder that it died out.

Most areas of the county also observed the tradition of taunting the Bed Churn, or Bed Churl. The 'Churn' was the last child to arrive at school, and the unfortunate one could expect physical abuse and humiliation. At Tideswell the somnolent child was hoisted onto a pole or cart-shaft called the Besom Stale and carried into the school with every last scrap of dignity abandoned. So maybe those spoil-sport teachers had a point after all...

Sometimes the Bed Churn suffered punishment at home. In Abney the poor child was thrown in the ash pit midden; and in Eyam everyone in the village had to suffer - to avoid being the Churn, boys would get up in the early hours of the morning and parade the streets with cacophonous pans, tins and horns, warning potential victims that it would be wise to rise.

Thomas Brushfield JP, correspondent to *The Reliquary* in 1865 commented:

'I must, as a faithful recorder, mention another Shrove Tuesday custom, and one that is still, I believe, observed - it is for an unengaged youth to kiss the first young single female he meets on that day. This custom is called 'Lousing', and the salutation is considered to be a sure presage of a union for life of the parties concerned. But that such a presage is not to be relied upon I am the living evidence.'
(See also Easter Monday)

COCK FLINGING - PLAYING CHICKEN

Street football was the main sport of the day (see below); and some far more dubious activities died out in the 18th century, including cock flinging. This involved the mass slaughter of poultry:

And on Shrove Tuesday when the bell does ring
We will go out at hens and cocks to fling.

Dr Clegg, Minister and High Peak physician, kept a diary in the early 18th century in which he recorded an incidence of this latter practice:

'On a Shrove Tuesday,
when ye young men of ye
upper end of ye school
were shooting with bows
and arrows at a cock,
and the rest of us made a
lane for the arrowes to
pass through, I put my head
a little too forward to see the
shott, and an arrow, shott by a
strong youth, (Mr George Brooks),
struck me on ye left temple, and made a
deep wound: it was at first thought mortal, but,
being committed to ye care of a skilful surgeon, it was
healed, through the mercy of God, but ye deep scar still remains.'

By the 20th century, if the sport survived at all, it was carried out with substitutes. Cotton bobbins were popular stand-ins; arrows had long ago been substituted by sticks; and the chicken only made its appearance as the top prize of the day.

SHROVETIDE FOOTBALL - HOOLIGANISM: THE EARLY YEARS

Ashbourne still stages its riotous Shrove Tuesday ball game, these days labouring under the title Ancient and Royal Shrovetide Football, the 'Royal' bit having been added in 1928 when the future Edward VIII 'turned up' the ball (i.e. threw it in the air to start the game). And then Prince Charles 'turned up' to continue the tradition in 2003.

At the onset the ball is carried ceremoniously from the Green Man and Black's Head Hotel through a wisely barricaded street. Once the scrum has formed, it is impossible to impose any rules or make any predictions. The ball is seldom kicked, and its movement up and down the town is more akin to a tight knot of defensive soldiers labouring across a particularly riotous battlefield. The goals are two and half miles apart, and the game is between the top and bottom halves of the town - the Uppies and Downies.

The game climaxes in the local river, Henmore Brook, and if a goal has, beyond all reasonable expectation, been scored before 5.30, a second ball is released into the maelstrom. If no goal has been scored by 10.30pm the police intervene, holding the ball in custody until Ash Wednesday, when the 'second half' commences.

Shrovetide football is all about letting off steam before the disciplines of austere Lent. The games have a long history, no doubt pre-dating the earliest recorded Ashbourne bout in 1400 and the early reference to community football on the streets of London in 1175.

Not surprisingly, notoriety has followed the practice down the centuries. In 1365 and again in 1388 it was prohibited as one of a number of pastimes deemed to interfere with archery practice.

King James I would not let his children play, claiming it was *'meeter for laming than making able the users thereof'.*

The Rev J.M.J. Fletcher wrote in 1911's *Derbyshire Archaeological Journal*:

'Derby was notorious, a hundred years ago, as a place where the whole town became violently excited over the annual contest. Shutters had to be put up and windows barricaded and it was not an uncommon thing for one of the contestants to swim across the river with the ball in his hands. At Ashbourne the authorities have only comparatively recently been able to check the rough horse-play of the annual

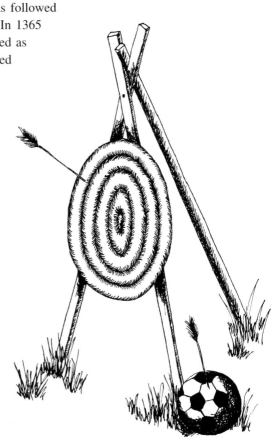

football festival. It is not surprising that in Tideswell... football should have been something to be reckoned with, and that the (Friendly) Society should regard injuries received in football playing or wrestling as in a sense self-inflicted.'

Receiving an injury during the game was, in the eyes of these early insurance-based Societies, placed in the same category as fighting or drunkenness - i.e. any claim for compensation would be laughed at.

The Derby game lingered until 1839, when there were scenes of unprecedented mayhem. The army intervened, the Riot act was read out, and the game never rose again. All that remains is a commemorative rhyme concerning the town's bells:

> *Pancakes and fritters, say All Saints and St Peter's,*
> *When will the ball come?, say the bells of St Alkmun',*
> *At Two they will throw, says St Werabo,*
> *Oh very well, says little St Michael.*

ASH WEDNESDAY - MATRIMONY: A PENITENT'S GUIDE

Ash Wednesday is the first day of Lent - the religiously enforced forty days of meat-free fasting and spiritual contemplation.

In reality, of course, it has always been a surfeit of pancakes followed by business-as-usual for most of the population, who feasted or fasted according to the dictates of the season, regardless of such spiritual considerations as Christ's forty days in the wilderness (the origin of the church's Lenten season).

So, a million miles from any hint of austerity... If no goal was scored in the Shrove Tuesday football at Ashbourne, the second half kicks off today. The other sport of the day is marbles - the season traditionally flicks off on Ash Wednesday.

Otherwise, it's off to church for a bit of good old-fashioned repentance. Ashes used to be sprinkled on sinners as they verbally repented - the origin, indeed, of the day's title. Anyone with nothing actually to repent, could attempt a spot of Lent marriage, bearing in mind the old rhyme: *Marry in Lent and you'll live to repent.*

MONSAL DALE FROM MONSAL HEAD

MARCH

1st - St. David's Day - EYAM

Most people have had a buttercup held under their chin to see 'if you like butter.' Children in Derbyshire used to do something far more complicated with daffodils (known in these parts as daffa-down-dillies). The flower-molesters would pluck out the stem with stamens intact, and thrust it up and down inside the flower's yellow trumpet, imitating the action of churning butter. This churning, as it was indeed called, was accompanied by the rhyme:

Churn, churn, butter churn,
Peter's at the iron gate
Waiting for a butter cake.

I mention this fact only because daffodils are supposed to flower for the first time on the feast of St David. But don't let the beauty of this moment or the rigours of churning divert your attention from the real business of this day - fleas.

On the first of March the women of Eyam used to sweep their doorsteps first thing in the morning, in a domestic ceremony known as dusting the fleas. It was said that if you failed to do this you would be plagued by fleas all year. This notion is backed up by a rather awkward rhyme which advises:

If from fleas you would be free,
On the first of March let your windows closed be.

On a more practical hands-on level, it is said that *'If you kill one flea in March you kill a hundred',* as this is their chief breeding season.

1st - COCKAINE PULLS HIS PAUNCHES - ROE DEER HUNTING

Roe deer hunting season commences on this day, according to *A Short Treatise on Hunting: Compyled for the delight of Noble men and Gentlemen, by Sir Thomas Cockaine, Knight, 1591* (see December 31st). This eminent Derbyshire man does not spare us the gory details, and nor will I (although I will update the spelling). Vegetarians are advised to look away now...

'When you have hunted the Hare all winter, and made your hounds very perfect, you may at the beginning of March give over the hunting thereof, and then begin to hunt the Roe in manner and form following...'

Cockaine now gives us full chase details, and we are advised that the roe, once caught and killed, should be saved from the ravages of the dogs:

...*'the Huntsman must first slit the legs and cut them off at the first joint; then must he slit the throat down the brisket to the nether end, and take the skin clean off; which done, he must slit his little belly, taking out the paunch with all the blood in the body, and lay it upon the skin with the four feet. If any town be near you must send for bread, for the better relief of your hounds to be broken in the blood, which being come, your Huntsman must let all the hounds forth of the couples, and hallowe them to the paunch, who must be very careful, that if any of his hounds be missing, he keep somewhat to relieve them withall, and also see diligently that every hound that be there hath some reward.'*

Horns are then to be blown, and the bulk of the carcass is given to a cook for larding and baking. Finally, floundering in the realms of mammalian physiology, Cockaine tells us:

'The scent of the Roe is far sweeter to hounds than any other chase: the reason is, he hath in his foreleg a little hole, whereat when he is hunted issueth out all his moisture; for he sweateth not outwardly as other Deer do, but only runneth forth at that hole. This chase may you well hunt until Whitsuntide.'

2nd - DOUBLE-CROSSING THE PLAGUE

The Glapwell Charters, a rich collection of 15th century parish records, give a grim sign of the times on this day in 1441. The entry includes a prayer to St Sebastian, invoking him for protection against the Plague which was raging at the time. All Saints had their particular specialist areas, and Sebastian, renowned for his courage, was the one called in to battle the dreaded Black Death.

The omnipresence of the Plague is hinted at in this 1498 entry in the Court Rolls of Temple Normanton: *'It is ordained that every tenant place the sign of the Holy Cross on his house before the next court under pain of 12d.'*

Significantly, we read in a 1513 entry: *'A pain laid on every tenant that they make double crosses on their houses and tofts before the next [court] under pain 6s 8d.'* Note that by this second entry the fine has increased enormously, and the cross deterrence has been doubled.

5th - THE SUM OF A MAN - JEDEDIAH BUXTON OF ELMTON

Some forms of autism are associated with natural mathematical genius. Jedediah Buxton of Elmton, born in 1707, certainly had the gift, even with no doctors to slap a label on him. Known to his friends as Jeddy, he managed to skip any schooling but was nevertheless able to go forth and multiply. No calculation was too vast for the man, and he was also able to assess the dimensions of land and buildings by eye alone. His well-deserved fame took him to London, and he became a legend in his own lifetime.

One of Jeddy's most famous calculations concerned the number of barleycorns that it would take to stretch end-to-end for eight miles. The answer, 1,520,640, amazed his audience at the Royal Society and the fact that they were unable to prove or disprove it did not dampen their enthusiasm.

Jeddy saved his most poignant sum for the end. He informed his employer, the Duke of Portland, that he would not be coming to work the following Thursday on account of an urgent tryst with Death. The Duke was dismissive and told his servants not to supply Mr Buxton with any more beer. Meanwhile, Jeddy said goodbye to all his friends; and, sure enough, on Thursday 5th March 1772 he was taken away to his decimal place in heaven.

6th - LARGE BIGNESS - NORTHERN LIGHTS

Not surprisingly, the Northern Lights are rarely seen in Derbyshire. There have, however, been isolated occurences. A set of seven lack-lustre verses printed under the title *'On the Strange and Wonderful Sight that was Seen in the Air on March 6th, 1716'* appears to describe an occurence of the Aurora Borealis at Hartington.

Twenty four days later something similar was reported at Chapel-en-le-Frith, and described by an observer as *'very terrible to behold'*. It was said to have lit the sky so brightly that locals could read books without the aid of candlelight. The reportage tells us how the lights *'streamed up like unto long picks of a large bigness'*; which is, we must assume, pretty huge.

10th - FERTILITY ON ICE - WEATHERLORE

This is a make or break day, according to weatherlore. As long as there is no ice on the 10th, the rest of the year will be fertile. If not... well, wave goodbye to bumper crops, new additions to the family, etc.

In general, the weather conditions in March are vital to the wellbeing of the germinating crops. Cold and dry is good, whereas warm and damp is disastrous. Hence such sayings as *'A peck of March dust is worth a King's ransom'*, *'March water is worse than a stain in cloth'*, and *'March damp and much warm will do the farmer much harm.'*

11th - SMALL TALK IN ASHFORD - MOLLY BRAY

Molly Bray the Ashford Dwarf, aka Owd Mally Bree, died on this day in 1811. Her belated obituary came in *The Reliquary*, 1863. Inevitably, much of the fascination with Molly stemmed not from her innate skills or eccentricities, but from the simple fact that she was very small. She did, however, take full advantage of her minor celebrity status.

Molly Bray was three feet high and lived in a now demolished cottage opposite the southern front of the church in Ashford-in-the-Water. In introducing its subject, *The Reliquary* speaks of the *'not altogether uneventful career of the lussus naturae'*.

She was never seen without the following items of clothing: a wide-brimmed hat, a red cloak or *'loose bedgown'*, a thin handkerchief over her head, and a breasted pinafore - *'both cloak and pinafore being extremely ragged and jagged at their nether extremities.'* She leaned on a knobbled stick, with a basket on her arm, and walked very slowly, pigeon-toed on *'marvelously small feet'*. She was also a prodigious clay pipe smoker, like many women of the time.

Not one to miss the opportunity of a hand-out, Molly *'had a peculiar habit of suddenly squatting down on the road, with her legs tucked up under her tailorwise; especially if any of the 'quality-folk' chanced to be rolling by in the carriages en route to Buxton, to whom she would make piteous appeals, her elfish appearance doubtless often extracting a coin which would have been denied an ordinary case or charity.'*

Molly Bray appears to have been a popular resident, although she was criticised for uncleanliness and slovenly living. As a result, although welcome in most houses it is recorded that householders would afterwards 'sweeten' the hearth where she had been squatting (never sitting, note). How many friendly neighbours today make their guests squat in the fireplace?

It is estimated that Molly was somewhere between 80 and 90 when she died. Death occurred in what *The Reliquary* describes as her 'hovel' - alone, she fell and struck her head on the fireplace. Fortunately, her threat to revisit her coffin-maker in the form of a 'boggart' if he failed to respect her precise instructions proved unnecessary (a boggart being a strange cross between a goblin and a ghost).

The obituary concludes: *'She was small, it is true, but her loss seemed to leave a larger void in the village she had lived in so long, much greater than would be felt at the death of one half of its full grown population.'*

15th - WHEN I GET TO PHOENIX - PEASLOW

On this day in 1716 Phoenix was engulfed, not by flames but by snow. She rose again on March 20th . This was 13-year-old Phoenix from Peak Forest. Resting at Peaslow on a journey home, she had been caught in typical Peak District weather -

'the most severe... snowing and driving rain that hath been seen in the memory of man', according to contemporary reportage. Stiff limbs and thirst were her only complaints when she was rescued from her makeshift ice shelter five days later.

Phoenix was luckier than others, like the famous Hope ice mummies (see January 14th); and spare a thought for 17th century John Warde, whose death is recorded in the Darley Dale registers as *'petrified with cold on ye moore'*.

18th - A PIG OF A FIND - TANSLEY MOOR

The Roman historian Pliny wrote in his epic work *Natural History*: *'In Britain, in the upper layers of the earth, lead is dug up in such plenty that a law was made forbidding its production above a certain quantity.'*

The British historian Camden claimed in his 16th century epic *Britannia* that Pliny was referring to Derbyshire, adding that *'Lead stones... are daily dug up in great abundance which they melt down with large wood fires upon those hills exposed to the west wind.'*

It is certainly true that the Romans mined the metal here, and had laws governing the size and price of iron 'pigs' (standard blocks of iron).

This is all vaguely interesting, you're probably thinking, but what has it got to do with March 18th? Well, on this day in 1894 a second-century AD Roman pig of lead was unearthed on Tansley Moor near Matlock by workmen preparing heathland for tillage. The pig's inscription read:

'(Property of) *Publius Rubrius Abascantus, from the mines of Lutudarum.'*

Lutudarum was a Roman lead and silver mine, thought to have been worked by prisoner slaves. From here the metal was usually carried along the Roman road to Chesterfield for sale.

Walter Kirkland, who reported for *Notes & Queries,* concluded:

'However great the improvements in smelting may have been in late years, one thing is certain - that the clumsy and ugly pigs of lead of the present day are not fit to be placed by the side of the artistically moulded and elegantly inscribed blocks of Roman workmanship in England.'

19th - St. Alkmund's Day - SAINT WITH A SPRING IN HIS TALE

This is the feast day of St. Alkmund's, the son of King Alchred of Northumbria. Father and son were forced into exile amongst the Picts of northern Britain during the era of Viking invasion and Danish rulers in the mid 8th century, although they made frequent attempts to win back their former territories.

Alkmund never made it to the throne himself, being killed by Northumbrian King Eardwulf in AD 800 at Northworthy (a royal estate now eaten up by the city of Derby, and a Roman settlement refortified and expanded by the Vikings later in the 9th century).

Soon afterwards miracles were reported at Alkmund's tomb in Lilleshall, Shropshire, and his body was later translated to Derby (the Church of St Alkmund's - no longer standing). Tradition maintains that the body was placed by the healing spring, which afterwards assumed the name of the saint, while the pall-bearers negotiated their passage through Derby's fortified walls.

The sarcophagus was hidden after the reformation, and lost altogether when a new church replaced the Mediaeval building in the 1840s. Unearthed during the church's final demolition in the brutal 1960s, it can now be seen in the city museum.

There have been one or two changes in Derby over the last 1000-plus years, and you won't find any traces of fortified city walls these days. Alkmund is still the city's patron saint, though, and the spring still bears his name. Many churches in the Derbyshire/Shropshire region are dedicated to this local hero.

20th - HOT EYRE

On this day in 1428 Richard Eyre was involved in a bloody brawl captured for posterity by contemporary reportage. Eyre, of Padley, was accused of murdering William Woodrove (Woodruffe) of Hope.

The incident occurred as the two friends, who also happened to be kinsmen, were riding from Chesterfield to Holme. An escalating argument resulted in William attacking Richard with his sword. The ensuing swordfight ended when Woodrove was wounded in the head, a blow from which he would die two days later.

A jury at the Criminal Sessions, however, decided that Eyre was not guilty. Instead they implicated one Peter Swordman - a handy enough name for the accused - of Brecknock in Wales, recorded as a labourer at Holme.

The incident is a randomly surviving fragment, but it is intriguing. For a start, such 'petty' cases were not normally the stuff of the Criminal Sessions, as this one was, but were put before a simple coroner's inquest. The man 'Peter Swordman' is conjured from nowhere, and the whole thing smacks of, at best, a rigged case; and, at worst, a set-up. This was the eve of the Wars of the Roses, when factions and tensions were running high. Eyre's political clout was able to sway the jury, and it comes as no surprise to

discover that he was from an influential local family.
Richard had fought at Agincourt in 1415 under the banner
of his father Nicholas Eyre of Hope, and married Joan
Padley, the sole heiress of Robert de Padley and his vast
estate in the Hope Valley.

The Eyres and Woodruffes were the most powerful
families in the region - the murder was probably
glossed over to save family alliances and reputations.
'Swordman' is not a Welsh name, and he may well have
been a 'John Doe', invented to satisfy the formalities of
justice. The Welsh, at the time, were generally disliked -
inventing a Welsh vagabond was therefore an ideal
scapegoat. Tantalisingly, though, the recorded proceedings
end with the statement: *'Thereupon the said Robert was thereof
quit, and the said Peter Swordman taken.'*

Anyway, the ruse and the political jiggery-pokery, if such
it was, succeeded. Richard Eyre remained the chief landowner
of the area, rebuilding Hathersage church, where he was buried
in 1459. His wife Joan followed him there in 1463.

23rd - AGREEABLE EXECUTIONS SHOCK HORROR - THE DERBY MERCURY

The *Derby Mercury* newspaper was launched this day in 1732. Newspapers had
succeeded in capturing the public imagination and were already becoming an
everyday part of middle class life. *The Mercury* was a weekly, printed by Samuel
Drewry. In the preface to his first edition he rambled:

*'I presume it will contain as much News, as any other paper published in the
neighbourhood; or, at least, as much that is material. The accounts of Goods
Exported and Imported, which take up so much room in some of our Country Weekly
Papers, is so stale and imperfect, (I might say false) that the publishing of 'em is
rather an imposition on the public than any real advantage; also the Diseases so
particularly mentioned in the London Bill of Mortality, with an account of the ages
of the Persons Dead, are what very few read over, which therefore I shall omit and
instead thereof, present my readers with something which I hope will be more
agreeable.'*

A firm pair of editorial scissors, perhaps? Drewry's notion of 'more agreeable'
is a matter of taste, the paper tending to specialise in criminal trial details, and
reproductions of ballad broadsheets giving lurid accounts of executions.

The editor was, indeed, from the cheap and cheerful end of the press, his other publications including the standard 'chap book' fodder of poorly printed children's stories, songs, almanacs, pseudo histories, riddles, etc., all presented on the very lowest quality paper. Samuel Drewry died in 1769, at which point his nephew John Drewry took over, renaming the paper *Drewry's Derby Mercury*.

25th - DYING TO GET MARRIED - WINNATS PASS

Peak Forest Chapel (destroyed in 1880) used to be the Gretna Green of England, until the church clamped down on its practices on this day in 1754.

The Chapel's heyday had been brief - in 1728 that the ministers here had assumed the title *'Principal Official and Judge in Spiritualities in the Peculiar Court of Peak Forest'*, recognising no superiors. Couples travelled from all over the country to *'Pay, marry, say nothing and go away'*, as the unofficial motto put it.

Not all the happy couples had a happy ending, though. In the 1750s a Scottish pair, having eloped and married at Peak Forest, were robbed and murdered at Winnats Pass in Castleton.

Their bones were finally discovered 10 years later, at which point the gory details were unravelled. One of the murderers, James Ashton of Castleton, confessed on his

WINNATS PASS

deathbed to assuage guilt. He revealed how he and four others (Nicholas Cock, Thomas Hall, John Bradshaw and Frank Butler) had overheard the newly weds talking in a pub, and realised that they carried a good deal of money.

The muggers pulled the unfortunates from their horses in Winnats and dragged them to a nearby barn, where they pocketed £200. Slitting the man's throat from ear to ear, they ignored the woman's pleas to be spared and turned out naked into the night (which itself hints at unpleasantries which contemporary reportage might have been coy about). Instead, they buried a miner's pick in her head.

The story claims that a 'frightful noise' so terrified the men that they failed to move the bodies for 48 hours. On the third night Ashton is reputed to have declared that the mysterious noise *'was only the devil, who would not hurt us'*, so the bodies were at last smuggled out to a secret grave.

Legend tidies the whole incident up, saying that the horses Ashton bought with his share of the money all died; that Cock fell to his doom from a precipice in Winnats; that Hall hanged himself in despair; that Bradshaw, revisiting the crime scene, was killed by a falling rock; and that Butler went mad and 'died miserably'.

The rock known as Lover's Leap in Ashwood Dale, a mile out of Buxton, has Peak Forest links too. A couple fleeing from their disapproving families were said to have leapt on horseback from this rock to the opposite side of the chasm. Impossibly wide, the pursuers did not dare to follow, and the couple were successfully wed at Peak Forest Chapel.

25th - Lady Day - BEAR NECESSITIES

Lady Day, which was New Year prior to 1752, is one of the best days in the year for spotting fairies (see October 31st and June 23rd). Dawn and dusk are thought to be the best times (not that it's anything to do with poor light and an over-active imagination).

One of Derbyshire's most interesting fairy residents is Hob Hurst, or plain Hob, commemorated in the county at four places named Hob Hurst's House. The one near Monsal Dale (also known as Hobthurst House) was mentioned by Thomas Brushfield, J.P., reflecting on the Ashford district at the turn of the 19th century. Writing in *The Reliquary,* July 1864, he says:

'These Hobthurst houses... were said to be inhabited by monster beings, named Hobthursts... who were believed to have such influence over dairy farms and dairy farming, as to be able to cause cows to go dry, or become barren, milk to turn sour, and cream to defy all the powers belonging to the art and mystery of churning, to be made to produce butter - yea, although the charm, else considered infallible, was said or sung over the laborious process. The words of the charm used on such occasions, are as follows -

> *Churn butter churn, churn butter churn*
> *Peter stands at our gate*
> *Waiting for a butter cake*
> *Churn, butter, churn!*

These Hobthursts were also supposed, during night-time, to open doors, arrange and remove crockery, and occasionally to lessen the stock of oatmeal, cheese or bacon, in the farmers' storerooms. All that was told about these beings, I believed to be true, as firmly as I believed in my own existence.'

Hobs were, it seems, a scapegoat for every ill. A horseshoe nailed to the door was sufficient to keep them away - the writer says he nailed one to his rabbit hutch for good measure.

Alternatively, a Hob could be made to perform good hard graft for the simple price of a bowl of cream. One miller in Monsal Dale was clearly not too keen on this unsolicited labour. Eschewing less hazardous options he managed to manhandle an irate bear into his mill one night. When the Hob came for his day's work, the bear attacked and the two fought noisily. No outcome is recorded, but afterwards the Hob was never seen again. We don't get to hear how the miller managed to evict the bear. (See also Good Friday).

25th - Lady Day - LANDOWNERS MUST BE KEPT ON A LEASE

On a more prosaic level, Lady Day was the time to hand over/collect rents and renew leases. This is broadly hinted in John Harestaffe of Sudbury Hall's eccentric *Rhyming Chronicle* (see December 1st):

> *Our Ladies day was come, tyme did require*
> *To sett such grounds as past from yeare to yeare.*

At this point in his narrative Harestaffe is in the middle of describing the protracted legal wranglings of Mary Vernon and some discontented rival landowners. With leases due for renewal, the guardians of Mary's niece Margaret were arguing that the land was up for grabs and should not return to Mary, but to Margaret and her guardians. Mary dug in her heels, refusing to recognise a court order against her, maintaining that the disputed lands - which had belonged to her dead brother-in-law - were hers forever. In the *Chronicle* at this point, the man responsible for the case, Justice Townsend, has had his bluff called, and:

> *....in this cause he would noe more contend,*
> *If she would harken to a friendlie end.*

As the Lady Day term approached, the rival parties met in London and found a *'friendlie end'*, settling the affair by marrying Mary's son Edward to the niece Margaret. It goes without saying that most Lady Day rents and leases were much more straightforward and prosaic than this.

27th - TOP TIP - HOWDEN MOORS

On this day in 1954, Tip the border collie was discovered on Howden Moors by the side of her dead master, Joseph Tagg. The two had set out from their home in Bamford fifteen weeks earlier, and the fact that Tip managed to survive the harsh winter on the moors is remarkable. She was nursed back to health by Tagg's niece Mrs. Thorp, but died just over ten months later.

She was awarded a medal by the National Canine Defence league. A commemoration stone, paid by public subscription, was erected near the site of Tip's epic vigil, and she was buried close by.

28th - ENGLISH GERMAN POLE CHARITY - RADBOURNE

In spite of his pan-European name, German Pole was born in Radbourne, Derbyshire. When he died on this day in 1683, his will leaped into action, establishing the German Pole Apprenticeship Charity.

Its aim was to rescue children - male or female and of 'honest parents' - from poverty by placing them in good trades. One child was to be taken annually - in May or June, said Pole - from Radbourne, Markeaton, Mackworth, Mickleover, Mercaston or Dalbury Lees, and placed under a master in Derby. After the apprenticeship (which lasted seven years, according to the Elizabethan Statute of Apprenticeships), the lucky young man or woman would be made '*a Burgess and ffreeman of and for the Corporation and Burrough of Derby.*'

The money for this magnanimous scheme came from land purchased with a lump sum left by Pole. If no suitable child could be located in any of the parishes, the £8 which would have been given to his/her new master was distributed amongst the poor. The Trustees added further stipulations later, declaring that children with the '3 Rs' - i.e. well-educated ones - were to be given preference.

The top five trades to which the children were apprenticed - and this gives us an interesting window into the era - were those of tailor, shoemaker, framework knitter (for making and seaming stockings, etc.), blacksmith and weaver. The first apprenticeship was handed out in 1685, and the last in 1753.

29th-31st - The Borrowing Days - LIVING IN BORROWED TIME

The three 'Borrowing Days' got their tag from some weird weatherlore which maintains that the end of March borrows three days from April. Or, as Sir Walter Scott put it, *'it is feigned that March had borrowed them from April to extend the sphere of his rougher sway.'* A traditional rhyme implies that April is happy to reciprocate:

> *March borrows of April*
> *Three days, and they are ill;*
> *April borrows of March again*
> *Three days of wind and rain.*

It is said that you must not lend or borrow anything on these days, as the item can later be used against you in witchcraft.

OTHER MARCH TRADITIONS

MOTHERING SUNDAY - TAKES THE CAKE

Mothering Sunday is now commonly known as Mother's Day, due to the influence of the Americans in the Second World War with their own Mother's Day on the second Sunday in May. Its other pseudonym is mid-Lent Sunday, it being the fourth Sabbath in Lent. The original feast has little to do with the cards-and-sentimentality of modern Mothering Sunday.

However, the gift of sweet foodstuffs has a respectable pedigree, the traditional dish of the day being Simnel cake. Recipes vary up and down the country, with currants, saffron and pastry crusts often featuring. An old legend tells how two characters called Simon and Nell once settled a culinary argument by first boiling and then baking their disputed cake mix, giving rise to the first Simnel.

PASSION SUNDAY - GOOD TASTE IN THE DOCK

This, the fifth Sunday in Lent, goes unobserved in Derbyshire; although throughout the north it was formerly observed as a day for over-indulging in beer and other intoxicants. Not a million miles away in West Yorkshire, the humble dock leaf is used as the basis for a traditional Passion Sunday dish called dock pudding. Take some dock, nettle, onion and oatmeal, mix to a green-grey slurry, and retire back to Derbyshire as quick as you can.

PALM SUNDAY - CROSS YOUR PALM WITH SALLOW

In some areas of the county this was the chosen day for visiting wells and going sugar-cupping (see Easter Sunday). Pins were dropped into a local well at Bradwell, and it was said that if this votive offering was not made, the children's sugar-cup drinking bottles would break on the following Sunday. More importantly, the Lady of the Well would not keep the water fresh and clean if she did not receive her tithe of pins. The first person to say *'ancient pagan beliefs surviving into modern day'* can join everyone else at the top of the class.

At Little Hucklow children used to decorate a spring called the Silver Well with a ring of pussy willow, in a simple ceremony akin to the more elaborate well dressings (see Ascension Day). Which link brings us neatly to the day's eponymous 'palm'...

Sallow, or pussy willow, being an early blossomer, was used in Derbyshire and the rest of Britain as palm substitute, and was commonly known as English Palm amongst country folk. Box, yew, hazel, common willow and daffodils ('Lent Lilies') were other alternatives, in the days before palm was easily available as an import from Spain.

Derbyshire place names commemorating the English Palm include Sawley and Sallewell, from the Old English *sahl*, sallow.

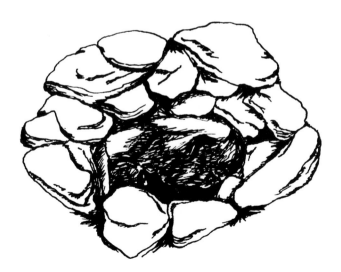

TISSINGTON HALL

APRIL

1st - MURDER TAKES ITS TOLL... - WARDLOW MIRES

April Fool's Day is still widely observed by children and adults alike. The oddity is that no-one really knows how the fleeting festival - which lasts from midnight to midday - originated. It may simply be a letting-off-steam remedy to the austerities of Easter, or it may be the tail-end of the Roman festival of Hilaria.

Unless, of course, that name is itself an April Fool's joke. Then again, it may have something to do with the Celtic god Lud, whose eight-day feast climaxed on April 1st (see April 30th for Lud).

Not that Anthony Lingard had much to laugh about on this day in 1815. Having murdered toll keeper Hannah Oliver, Lingard's hanged body was placed in the gibbet at Wardlow Mires, at a site still known as Gibbet Field.

After investigating a noisy tailback at the area's long-gone toll gate, the barmaid of the nearby Three Stags' Heads Inn discovered Hannah's murdered body at the toll-keeper's cottage, minus a pair of red shoes. This proved to be the sole clue in the murder hunt, but when the footwear was brought to heel at the home of Anthony Lingard, he was caught red footed.

Bizarrely, their original maker was able to prove that they had belonged to Hannah Oliver. The shoemaker recalled using a piece of packing in the sole featuring the words 'Commit no Crime', and when he took the shoes apart, the evidence was found.

Lingard was strung up twice, having the dubious honour of undergoing bodily decay in Derbyshire's last gibbet. Toll-keepers and bar staff complained about the eerie rattling of bones, and William Newton (see November 3rd) wrote a poem condemning the punishment. The poem appears to have been instrumental in the abolition of gibbets.

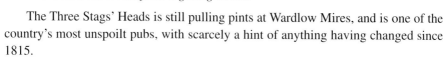

> ...If crime demand it, let the offender die,
> But let no more the Gibbet brave the sky;
> No more let vengeance on the dead be hurled,
> But hide the victim from a gazing world.

The Three Stags' Heads is still pulling pints at Wardlow Mires, and is one of the country's most unspoilt pubs, with scarcely a hint of anything having changed since 1815.

2nd - WOOLLY THINKING - TISSINGTON

In the 17th century an Act of Parliament dictated that everyone should be buried in a woollen shroud - an unsubtle and sure-fire way of supporting the English wool industry. There were automatic fines for any corpse seen to be breaking this law. Church registers from Tissington record a good example of this, and it seems that people could choose between burying the dead in wool or paying £5 and choosing their own material:

2nd April, 1683 - ...Whereas the late Mr. William P- was buried in linen contrary to the late Act of Parliament for burying in wool , the penalty of five pounds according to the said Act was paid out, half to the informers and half to the poor of Tissington.

3rd - BEYOND APRIL SHOWERS - WEATHERLORE

Back in the land of the living, April fog precipitates June rain. Weatherlore for the first three days of the month serves up this homely rhyme:

If the first three days of April be foggy,
Rain in June will make the lanes boggy.

In similar vein, you might like to reflect on such perennial classics as: *April showers bring May flowers*; *An April fish is a dainty dish*; and *April floods carry off frogs and their broods.*

Eschewing rhyme, we are also told to *Never trust an April sunshine*; warned that *A windy April is death to little pigs*; and assured that *Snow in April is manure*. The men mentioned on April 22nd would definitely not agree with that last one; but then just how many of these weather proverbs are a pile of April snow?

8th - POSTHUMOUS BIGAMY - BAKEWELL

The fact that Bakewell worthy John Dale married twice gave an anonymous epitaph writer an excuse to bring a dash of verbose humour to his chisel. The following can be read in Bakewell church:

Know posterity that on the 8th of April in the year of grace 1757 the rambling remains of the abovesaid John Dale were in the 88th year of his pilgrimage laid upon his two wives. This thing in life might raise some jealousie: Here all three lye together lovingly, but from embraces here no pleasure flows. Alike here are all human joys and woes. Here Sarah's chiding John no longer hears and old John's rambling Sarah no more fears, a period's come to all their toilsome lives, the goodman's quiet, still are both his wives.

10th - LANCASTER BOMBSHELL - ENCLOSURE RIOTS

One day you're grazing your livestock on common land like umpteen generations before you; the next day someone fences it off and informs you that you're trespassing.

This was the injustice that fired the country's many anti-enclosure riots between the 16th and 19th centuries. In 1569 there was an early uprising at Chinley, where the surrounding countryside had been grabbed by the Duchy of Lancaster. The rioters gathered a makeshift armoury of pitchforks, staves, clubs, mattocks, spades, etc., and pulled down the offending fences and newly erected buildings.

The movement gathered force throughout the High Peak, and the anti-enclosure movement in this part of the world became so severe that the armed forces were told to intervene, resulting in mass arrests, trials, ignominy for the commoners and more wealth for those who already had plenty of it.

Worse was to come, and under George III (1760-1820) an incredible 2,300 Enclosure Acts changed the face of the English landscape forever.

An essay on the subject by Rev. Charles Kerry, published in 1899's *Derbyshire Archaeological Journal,* comments, with a mixture of eulogy and melancholy:

'The disturbance has long ago subsided, and the spirits, then so much moved and swayed by passion and contending interests have passed away; the heart-burnings have ceased, and the present villagers may not even know that their little hamlet, now so quiet, was once the scene of so much contention. From (the) original and authentic sources, we can see our ancestors in their struggles, and their yearnings for justice and for right; we mark their crude ideas, and note our own advancement; and if it were only for this - to afford us the feeling of contentment that our lot is cast in better times - these various publications of the Society will have contributed to some good end.'

11th - ASHOVER RINGS BONAPARTE

Napoleon Bonaparte abdicated on this day in 1814, and was subsequently imprisoned on Elba. A year later he was back in charge of the French army and facing his proper nemesis at Waterloo.

The good folk of Ashover were not to know of this, however. After the news of his apparent defeat in 1814 reached the village the church bells rang out joyfully. So joyfully, in fact, that the C-sharp bell broke. It was recast afterwards, with the no-nonsense inscription:

'The old bell rung the fall of Bonaparte and broke, April 1814'.

12th - MAIDENS' GARLANDS - THE FIRST PAPER HANDKERCHIEFS

When Ann Howard of Ashford-in-the-Water died on this day in 1747, aged 21, posterity decided to award her the obscure consolation prize of a Maiden's Garland, or Maiden's Crant.

These 3 dimensional commemorative rosettes of paper flowers, ribbons, handkerchiefs and gloves were made by the friends of girls who died before marriage, and Ann's just happens to have survived.

Richard Keene in his 1858 *Ramble Over Derbyshire Hills and Dales*, having visited Ashford, notes that the garlands *'are becoming extremely rare in our county churches'*.

18th century poet Anne Seward, one-time Eyam resident, commemorated the garlands she had seen in her youth with these lines:

> *Now the low beams with paper garlands hung,*
> *In memory of some village youth or maid,*
> *Draws the soft tear, from thrill'd remembrance sprung;*
> *How oft my childhood marked that tribute paid!*

> *The gloves suspended by the garland's side,*
> *White as its snowy feathers with ribbands tied,*
> *Dear village! Long these wreaths funereal spread,*
> *Simple memorial of the early dead.*

Keene recalls seeing garlands in Ilam church, and notes that during his rambles in Hathersage: *'We saw, at a lone house, a garland stretched across the road, with a wreath and a pair of gloves cut in paper suspended from the centre'*.

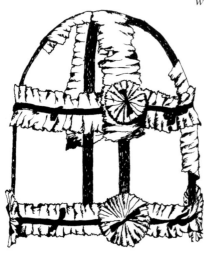

Clearly, this was not just a church observance, but a form of personal mourning, an ostentatious variant on leaving the curtains drawn in a house that has recently suffered a bereavement.

After visiting Crich church, the early 18th century historian Adam Wolley, of Riber near Matlock, wrote: *'The pillars continue to be hung with garlands in honor of young maidens who died unmarried.'*

The withered garlands still hang their melancholy heads at Ashford and Ilam, along with Matlock and Trusley. (See December 9th).

13th - HEIRS AND GRACES - HADDON HALL

Henry de Vernon of Haddon died on this day in 1515. Destined, or so it seemed, for great political influence, Vernon had made the right gamble in the civil wars, siding with Henry Tudor and lending a hand at the all-important Battle of Bosworth in 1485. This, and his marriage to Anne, daughter of the Earl of Shrewsbury, made him one of the most powerful men in England in the early 16th century.

Vernon was appointed governor to the young Prince Arthur and was established as such on April 13th 1492. Arthur was the eldest son of the victorious Henry Tudor (Henry VII), the name being a symbolic nod to that great mythical leader of the Britons. Unfortunately Britain was denied its second King Arthur, as the prince died young and the throne (plus Arthur's wife Katherine of Aragon) passed to the tenure of Henry Tudor's second son, Henry VIII.

Henry Vernon's influence was snatched away, but the wealth remained, most of it stored up in Haddon Hall. Of the little wealth he willed away from the Hall, some went to buy *'The Big Bell'* for the church in the town of Tonge in Shropshire, where Vernon's wife was buried. It was installed *'for the tolling of it when any Vernon comes to town'*. This must have been very inconvenient for any Vernon sneaking back to Tong after a clandestine night on the tiles.

It is unknown whether Henry de Vernon had any hand in the long tunnel which, according to folklore, stretches between Haddon Hall and Bakewell Church. This is one of many apocryphal tunnels running obscurely under the Derbyshire subsoil. Human imagination clearly enjoys the idea of such unlikely routeways existing.

14th - YEAR ON A STICK - ALMANACS

Before Henry VIII's brutal Reformation in the 16th century, the Almanac - aka Runestick, Rune Stock, Rune Stave, Prime Stave or Messe-dag (Mass Day) Stave - was kept in most churches and many households.

The device is a combined calendar and mnemonic, in the form of a notched log or staff. Short notches mark weekdays, with a seventh longer one for every Sunday.

April 14th is the pivotal day which marks the switch from winter to summer on the older, shorter staves. The winter months were marked on one side, summer's on the other.

Almanacs became more complex over time, and Saints' Days (the original 'holy' days) were marked with a symbol representing that saint. For example, an anchor was used for Clement, a wheel for Catherine and a three-branched candle for Nicholas, all tying in with aspects of their respective legends. Others, such as the goose used for Michael, reflected secular custom - in this case, the goose traditionally roasted and devoured at Michaelmas (September 29th).

April 14th on the Almanac, in addition to being the winter-summer junction, was often marked as the feast of Saints Tiburtius and Valerianus. A reader would know that if it snows on this day the country is in for nine more snowfalls before midsummer.

April 16th, the feast of St Magnus, is denoted by a pickaxe, indicating that fieldwork should now commence. The Runestick was meant to jog the memory - and if all else failed you could hit someone over the head with it.

The pagan Anglo Saxons introduced these Almanacs to the island, based on Scandinavian models. The earliest ones were very simple, marking the phases of the moon and the major holidays, hence the word 'Almanac', from Saxon al-mon-aght, *'heed all moons'.*

The last models were made in the 17th century, by which time the aide memoire was a four-sided device, with one season per side - the 'Clog Almanac'. The best surviving examples are from Staffordshire. An anonymous writer travelling through Derbyshire in 1709 noted in Buxton: *'A gentleman that was travelling showed me an Almanack of the Danish invention. It was 2 foot long 4 square and not like what Dr Plot met in Staffordshire yet essentially the same.'*

The Runesticks marked today as the beginning of summer. This concept is backed by the fact that April 14th is known - or was in previous generations - as First Cuckoo Day. Cuckoos are the harbingers of summer, and this was the day when they were expected to call for the first time. In Derbyshire the lore relating to this is specific. It is said that if your pockets contain gold coins when you first hear the bird, you will have plenty of that metal; if you have silver, you will have sufficient; if you have copper, you will never be without. Slightly cryptic, but the message is very much 'business as usual'. The chances of the modern wayfarer carrying gold coin are, of course, slim.

Then again, it is also said that if the cuckoo calls from the right, it brings good luck. If it calls from the left, you'll wish you'd brought a bit of gold along as consolation.

15th - REAL AIL - BOWDEN HALL

Let this be a warning to all you inveterate revellers. On this day in 1681, Thomas Bowden of Bowden Hall near Chapel-en-le-Frith wined and dined himself and two friends into an early grave. After dinner the party uncorked a few bottles of the not-so-good stuff, and after indulging excessively in their alcoholic revelries, they died.

Had they survived they would doubtless have blamed the curry.

18th - THE ORIGIN OF THE DARWINS - BREADSALL

Erasmus 'Grandfather of Charles' Darwin, died on this day in 1802. He lived for many years at Breadsall Priory (which his own prematurely deceased son, another Erasmus, bequeathed him in his will). Erasmus senior was a man of great learning, and his tomb in the church at Breadsall sings these praises:

'*Of the rare union of Talents which so eminently distinguished him as a Physician, a Poet and Philosopher His writings remain a public and unfading testimony.*'

Darwin was not without his critics, however. Derbyshire-born poet, Anne Seward, wrote an entire book, *The Life of Dr Darwin*, as a full-frontal attack on the old man. The odd thing is that Anne was generally fêted for her kindness and compassion; although she appears to have been very conceited and petulant too.

On the whole, however, Darwin was a popular and respected figure, and something of a radical in his pursuit of social and parliamentary reform, and in his vocal support of the French and American Revolutions. The poet Coleridge described him as '*the first literary character in Europe*'.

19th - OUT OF PLACE IN THE PUB - DERBY

Let this be yet another warning to all you inveterate revellers. On this day in 1636, William Huberd, the Sexton of St Werburgh Church in Derby, was given an official final warning for failing to succumb to the delights of sobriety.

The church's records state: '*Memorandum - it is this day Ordered by the parishioners Wm Huberd now Sexton is contemned, that if said Wm still frequent alehouses or be Drunk that then he shall be put out of his place.*'

Unfortunately, like most drunken bouts this story ends in a blank, and we don't get to hear whether the parishioners' wish was granted.

22nd - DRINKS, WITH ICE - GARDOM'S EDGE

Perhaps it is due to the first hints of fine weather and the rising of the sap, but there's something about April that causes men to engage in ill-advised adventures with the fruits of Bacchus and Ceres.

Having poured two cautionary draughts of the strong stuff on the 15th and 18th, the 22nd has no less than three victims of the demon drink.

At Gardom's Edge east of Baslow there are three commemorative cairns in a sobering straight line. These mark the spots where three South Yorkshire clergymen collapsed after attending the funeral of Eyam curate Ralph Rigby on this day in 1740.

Staggering home through the snow after drinking heartily to Rigby's memory, the men lost their way on Eastmoor and eventually keeled over. A shepherd found them the following day, by which time only one remained alive.

24th - GIVE US OUR TRESPASSES - THE NATIONAL PARK

This is a red letter day in the Peak District - the day when, in 1932, the Mass Trespass on Kinder Scout finally brought the issue of selfish land ownership and rights of way into the headlines.

In spite of the predictable outrage of landowners and gamekeepers, the commoners got their boots muddy on the moorlands, kick-starting the negotiations which led to the establishment of the country's first National Park in 1951. Okay, it took 19 years, and we 21st century hikers now take it for granted; but it was a triumph, ushering in a new era and genre of leisure for the masses.

24th - St Mark's Eve - WRAITH AGAINST TIME

St Mark's Eve is the day when the not-quite-dead roam the earth. It is said that if you keep vigil near a church, the wraiths of those locals doomed to grave illness over the coming year will parade into the church. The ones who will recover re-emerge soon afterwards, but all the ones locked inside will be decorating God's Acre in the near future.

This is a prime night for divination in general. Sleep with three blades of grass from a south facing grave under your pillow, and you will dream of a future lover. The peckish spirit of your lover-to-be can be summoned if you lay the table at midnight. Easiest of all, simply sit in a barn and your future spouse will walk in.

Beware, though, as this is one of the nights when Satan rides abroad. He is overseeing the annual blossoming and seeding of fern (also known as Devil's Harvest), which cycle it accomplishes in just 24 hours.

The plant has microscopic spores rather than seeds; but our ancestors didn't know that, and would happily assure you that if you can catch fern seed between two pewter plates, you will become as wise as the Devil.

25th - St Mark's Day - SPICE HOPPER

If you haven't seeded your land by the 25th it's too late. This day marks the end of Spring sowing and used to be celebrated with a small feast for farm labourers, which was sometimes known as Hopper Cake Night. A 'hopper' in this case is a seed basket, and spiced cakes were the traditional fodder, usually served with, or in, beer. (See November 11th). A clumsily metered Derbyshire lore sums it up:

> *On St Mark's Day*
> *A good farmer must put his seed hopper away.*

29th - PREPARING FOR AN ANTI-SOCIAL DIET

According to an old rhyme:

> *Set garlic and beans on St Edmund the King,*
> *The moon on the wane thereof hangeth a thing.*

It is sometimes best not to argue with these things. Suffice to say this rhyme refers to the feast of the translation of Edmund the Martyr - not his main feast day on November 20th, (unless you don't like garlic and beans).

Bean-setting also happens to be the name of a traditional Morris tune; and if you wait until May 1st you're in with a good chance of seeing the dancers in action.

30th - A LOAD OF HOLLYHOCKS - BELTANE

This is May Eve, the festival of Beltane. In the Celtic calendar it was the eve of summer, when the hag-like goddess of winter transformed herself into the beautiful goddess of growth and plenty. In Derbyshire it was customary to go May Birching today. The birchers would travel through their locality with sprigs from different trees, placing them on houses as they saw fit.

Each plant had its significance, usually based on a simple bit of rhyming. For example, pear meant 'fair', lime meant 'prime', thorn was 'scorn', holly was 'folly' and briar declared 'liar'. The worst insults were gorse which represented 'whores', and nut which equalled 'slut'.

More obscurely, wicken (rowan) symbolised 'chicken', which in this case was an amorous compliment (as in chick, or chuck - the modern equivalent would be 'babe').

This notion of a 'Language of Flowers' was very popular in Victorian England, when dozens of flowers were roped into the iconography, giving scope for the most complex of messages and responses. The 'rhymes' concept, understandably, could only ever have limited scope. After all, by this time the rhododendron had been introduced to Britain.

Fairies are out and about tonight and tomorrow, so protect yourself by gathering some elder leaves. These are also said to heal wounds, and are so powerful that the fairies themselves use them as protection against evil spirits. John Evelyn in his 1706 *Sylva, or a Discourse on Forest Trees,* called elder *'a kind of Catholicon against all Infirmities whatever.'*

May Eve Dew is a great healer too, and this is the only night when you can bottle it. In Eyam and the surrounding villages sick children used to be washed with the stuff.

If you don't believe in fairies but your future love life is troubling you, take a snail, place it on a pewter plate and be patient. It will, at its own go-slow pace, trace the initials of your future lover in the patterns of its slime.

Dragons are not much of a menace these days, but the county still has a few scars to show for past encounters with the reptilian monsters. The 'worm' in Wormhill and the 'drake' (dragon) in Drake Low commemorate local specimens. Celtic British folklore used to maintain that the fighting of two dragons on May Eve caused such terrible roars and shrieks that the entire country was blighted. Mythical god King Lud managed to capture the dragons by luring them into a mead-filled pit, after which he buried them under Mount Snowdon.

EASTER TRADITIONS

GOOD FRIDAY - CHRISTIANITY DOUBLE CROSSED

Derbyshire tradition maintains that it is unlucky to work horses on this day. It is also unlucky to burn elder wood; although in general this tree is said to harbour benevolent spirits. You should still ask the tree's permission if you want to cut some of its wood, though. As far as I can tell, the incidence of trees refusing the harvest is zero; but it's just as well to be polite.

Once the fuel is gathered - whichever type you opt for - the traditional hot-cross buns can be baked. Thanks to the season-busting rule of the mighty Supermarket, these delicacies are now available all year round. It is worth mentioning, however, that those splendid crosses on the top of the buns predate Christianity. The Greeks and Ancient Egyptians are thought to have etched their holy cakes with the very same symbol.

Various games used to kick off on Good Friday, in days when these things were strictly seasonal. Skipping and shuttlecock (badminton) were favourites with the girls, while the boys went in for whip and top and marbles, the latter, having commenced on Ash Wednesday, reaches its climax on Good Friday.

Ordinary work tended to be laid aside today. Lead miners in Bradwell refused to work underground on such a holy feast, but would acquiesce to working above ground, if pushed.

Thurst Hole or Hob's Thirst House, is a cave and spring in Deep Dale near Buxton. It is said that its resident Hob, a species of hobgoblin, was the originator of the magic which makes the spring curative. It only has this magical property on Good Friday, however. The 'thirst' element of the cave's name seems to tie in with the idea of drinking; but this is mere etymological skulduggery. 'Hob Thirst' comes from Hobthrust or Hob Hurst, being the name of this particular species of fairy. The 'hurst' part of the name signifies that the fairy lives in woodland.

Deep Dale was once thought to be a popular haunt for fairies in general. Small clay pipes unearthed in the nearby fields were thought to be their smoking detritus. There are other sites called 'Hob Hurst House' in the county, including ones in Monsal Dale, the Manifold Valley, and one on the moors above Chatsworth. (See March 25th).

EASTER SUNDAY - WATER SPORTS

In the early hours of Easter Sunday morning a mermaid appears at Mermaid's Pool below Kinder Scout. To see her is a guarantee of immortality, which surely has to be worth the brisk climb involved. Aaron Ashton of Hayfield died at 104 in 1855, and he used to keep his tryst with the mermaid every Easter Eve. Okay, it wasn't exactly immortality, but not a bad innings nevertheless; and Aaron also managed to escape the Battle of Bunker's Hill in the American War of Independence with nothing more than a good wounding. Male visitors should keep a safe distance, however. One strand of legend maintains that the mermaid likes nothing better than to drag men to a watery grave.

On a less fantastical aquatic theme, this is a day for adding a lump or two to your water supply. Sugar cupping was widely - you might accurately say religiously - observed in many places, including Ashford-in-the-Water. At its simplest the tradition involved a cup of sugar topped up with water from the local spring. At

Ashford the favoured site was Sinners' Well, in a dell beneath Great Shacklow. Thomas Brushfield JP, writing in 1864, declares *'The custom of drinking the sugar and water is almost, if not entirely, abandoned.'* (See Whitsun, below).

At Tideswell the favourite site for sugar cupping was the Dropping Tor, where sweet-toothed adherents would catch the water as it fell from the rock. At Castleton the custom was called Shak' Bottle. The water was brought from the Well of Our Lady at the top of Cave Dale on Good Friday, and the liquorice was steeped in it until the Sunday and sipped during the church service. The custom took place on Whit Monday in Chapel-en-le-Frith. (See Whit Monday)

In Castleton folk used to congregate at the top of Castle Hill at sunrise, to see the sun perform an Easter Sunday dance. The 'dancing' is an occasional optical illusion, but was said to be the sun celebrating the rebirth of Christ.

EASTER MONDAY - A LOUSY ARRANGEMENT

Carrying on from the previous day's sugar cupping, children would often carry their bottles around their necks all day on Easter Monday, begging sugar or sweets from neighbours.

Today was known as Unlousing Day in the Peak District. Girls were seized, kissed, and hoisted aloft by the unruly boys. It was said to reflect the 'rising' of Christ, but that sounds like a flimsy excuse for a spot of manhandling and groping. On Easter Tuesday the girls could return the dubious compliment. To 'unlouse' meant to set free - i.e. from the strictures of the Lent season. (See Shrove Tuesday).

EASTER MONDAY - JUST ROLL WITH IT

In the spirit of traditional Easter pastimes, Carsington Water hosts an Easter Egg Hunt on Easter Monday. The event is now firmly established in the calendar, and if you scour the tourist press you should be able to track down similar revivals elsewhere.

In a county that boasts impressive hills in its northern reaches, an Egg Rolling revival is long overdue. Similar events, featuring brightly painted hard-boiled eggs and formidable gradients, can be enjoyed at Fountains Abbey in North Yorkshire and at Preston in Lancashire. The latter event attracts around 40,000 people every year, a figure that should give Derbyshire event organisers something to chew on. 40,000 eggs, to be precise.

EASTER TUESDAY - RACERS START TO FLAGG

This is the day for Flagg Races at Flagg Moor (off the A515 Buxton to Ashbourne road). It is a point-to-point horse race across the limestone uplands, organised by the High Peak Harriers. The first of the six races gets under starter's orders at 2pm. The going is rough, the weather is often bleak, and it is not unknown for no horse to complete the race.

TITHES - CLOVE AND HOOF

Church tithes fell due at Easter, generally. The accepted reason was that the collected money would pay for the Eucharist ingredients throughout the year. The fee in the 17th century was about 2d on average; although in much of the High Peak it seems to have been more taxing.

For example, in the church tithe records at Hope 6d is the lowest payment. Special Easter dues were often exacted too, in the form of a livestock tax. In Hope this was an exorbitant 2d per cow and 1/2d per calf. Shepherds gave 1d per flock, and beekeepers 2d. This was all in addition to the additional tithes of goods - i.e. of honey, wool, meat, etc., which the church also claimed. Poultry farmers had to donate two eggs per hen and three eggs per cock.

Even more covetously, in the High Peak every tenth swarm of bees in a locality belonged by default to the local Vicar. A penny was paid for every piece of plough-land too (although there are not so many of those in the High Peak).

Vicars were usually the recipients of the hard cash tithes; but in the Peak it had been the practice since the reign of King John for the loot to be collected by an official from the Dean and Chapter of Lichfield Cathedral. Hope, over the three years 1658-60, raised £35 and 3 shillings by these tithes.

Some rents were mere token gestures, consisting of a rose or a clove, for example. Church records are full of these pieces of ancient historical favouritism - for example, '1 clove gilly-flower, payable at Easter', is the recorded rent on some land at Eckington, in 1252. (See June 24th).

P.S. - April is the usual month for the meeting of the Great Barmote Court of the Soke and Wapentake of Wirksworth. See October 10th for details.

HOPE MARKET CROSS

MAY

1st - May Day - PAIL INTO SIGNIFICANCE

Robin Hood used to feature in May Day parades, taking on the mantle of Jack-in-the-Green, the pagan spirit of summer and greenery. With a folkloric stamping ground stretching from South Yorkshire to Nottinghamshire, Robin was certainly no stranger to Derbyshire. Indeed, one tradition maintains that he was born at Chellaston, and the local Robin Wood may be a commemoration, or may be local legend's starting point.

Robin married Maid Marian under the ancient yew tree in Doveridge churchyard, estimated to be in excess of 1,400 years old. Other obscure Robin memorials include Robin Hood's Cave on Stanage Edge; Robin Hood's Cross on Abney Moor; Robin Hood's Stoop on Offerton Moor; Robin Hood's Picking Rods, two standing stones near Chisworth; and Robin Hood's Croft and Robin Hood's Moss near the Derwent and Ladybower reservoirs.

With or without Robin Hood, May Day was a day for dancing in celebration of the newly arrived summer - never mind all that June 21st stuff. At Eyam the entire village used to dance through the streets, and bunches of flowers and greenery were hung from windows.

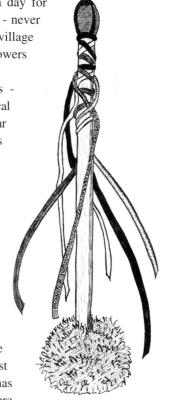

Many towns hold revived May Queen parades - Hayfield's is one of the most well-known, and the local song and air, *Humours of Hayfield Fair*, is a popular Maypole and Morris dancing tune. May Queen fans should note, however, that most of these festivities now fall on the ubiquitous Bank Holiday weekend rather than May 1st.

Many villages in Derbyshire had a variation called kit dressing. This custom survived longest in Baslow, where the kits - small milk pails - were decorated with flowers and ribbons and paraded through the streets by girls, to the music of an all-male band. Before you could say the word 'matchmaking', there was an evening dance at which the couples would attempt to pair off.

May Eve/May Day is one of the best times of the year for seeking out curative wells. One of the most intriguing of these is the Dewric Well at Bretton. It has a fertility effect for any woman who takes a drink there.

If you believe everything you read, ancient well-worship continues to this day in the Longdendale region of the Peak District. Pagan practices are said to have lingered here, and May 1st is the most important day of the ritual year. Wells are garlanded, fires are lit, and stone heads are worshipped. Allegedly.

Festivities were far from the minds of Derbyshire folk back in 1048. The winter had been long and severe, and according to an entry in the Anglo-Saxon Chronicle:

'In this year on May 1 there was an earthquake in many places, at Worcester, Droitwich, Derby and elsewhere. There was also a great mortality of men and cattle, and wild fires which spread over Derbyshire and other places did great damage.'

4th - PULLING A FAST ONE - ANNE MOORE OF TUTBURY

I, Anne Moore of Tutbury, humbly asking pardon of all persons whom I have attempted to deceive and impose upon, and above all, with unfeigned sorrow and contrition imploring the divine mercy and forgiveness of that God whom I have greatly offended, do most solemnly declare that I have occasionally taken sustenance for the last six years.

This is the confession that Ashbourne-born Anne Moore was forced to sign on this day in 1813, having made herself famous by pretending to undergo a six year holy fast. The public fascination with fasting damsels was itself very unhealthy, and the fact that Anne was sent to prison for collecting money by deception seems very unfair. Anyone daft enough to believe a woman could exist on air and prayer for six years deserves to be fleeced; and the £250 she managed to amass over that time was hardly a fortune.

Anne had planned the deception in 1807, aged 46, based on the example of Martha Taylor (see June 12th), and had eaten food smuggled in by her own daughter. Only when a truth-hungry committee was formed to test the fast was Anne's free lunch over. After nine days she was on the verge of death, and the above confession was the result.

8th - THE DERBYSHIRE EVE - SARAH ROSE OF HOPE

Born on this day in 1713, Sarah Rose is the anti-smoking lobby's nightmare. She smoked her clay pipe almost constantly and died at the age of 106, with 214 living descendants. This means that by now most of the indigenous Derbyshire population are probably related to her.

She was born in Glossop and spent most of her life in Hope, where she died. Having raised her own huge family, at the age of 90 she became housekeeper to one of her sons when his wife died. Since her ninth decade she had been toothless, and a touch blind and deaf. Bizarrely, at the age of 102 her senses returned, and she cut a new set of teeth. This rejuvenation only lasted two years, however, after which the new teeth fell out and she went into decline, dying in 1819.

Living through the reign of the four Georges, Sarah was born in the year before the death of Anne, last of the Stuarts, and died in the year Queen Victoria was born.

8th - DEATH: LONG TERM RESIDENT - DERBY WORKHOUSE

Prior to the more enlightened policies of the late 20th century, the Workhouse was the destination of people lacking the money to support themselves. Many who wound up in the Workhouse finished their days there - given the environment of insufficient food and hard work, it was hardly surprising.

The governor of the Derby Workhouse was all too aware of the grim presence of Death when he filed this report on May 23rd 1840:

'Would call the serious attention of the Board on the want of a proper ventilated place to lay out the Dead. Hitherto we have occupied first one and then another Refractory Ward for that purpose, but for want of proper Ventilation have found them very obnoxious on account of the putrid effluvia being so confined. Especially from two Bodies... I was very ill most of this day on consequence of going in with the Men who took the Measure for the Coffins. And I do recommend also that something should be allowed to the persons who wash the Dead and put them in their Coffins to prevent their being taken ill while performing that office, as I am always obliged to take some stimulant at my own expense or I should certainly not be able to attend during such painfull seasons.' (See also May 23rd)

9th - LEICESTER SQUARE MEAL

Landowners come in all sizes and humours, from the squalid and tight-fisted to the absurdly rich and generous, and any combination thereof. At the squalid end of the scale sits John Tupman. A brief note in the Court Rolls of Temple Normanton made on this day in 1489 indicates that things must have been getting particularly bad with his properties. The court order reads *'John Tupman to repair his houses under pain of 6s 8d'*. Tupman's heirs are, sadly, thriving in the 21st century.

At the other end of the scale is the all-wining, all-dining Earl of Shrewsbury. On this day in 1577, Queen Elizabeth I wrote to the him at his Buxton lodgings, thanking him for recently entertaining her favourite courtier, the Earl of Leicester (Lord Dudley). In the letter she notes with some concern that Leicester is looking somewhat out of shape, and she blames Shrewsbury for over-feeding him. Her words are a wonderful mixture of affection, concern, gentle rebuke and stand-up comedy:

'As to the large allowance of diet they gave him must remain their debtor, but advises in future that he should not be allowed by the day more than two ounces of

flesh, the twentieth part of a pint of wine to comfort his stomach, but as much St Anne's water as he listeth; on festival days to have for his dinner the shoulder of a wren, and for supper the leg of the same.'

11th - Old May Eve - RISKING A SLOE DEATH

Some people argue that old May Eve is the best time for visiting curative wells, rather than the 'new' May Eve.

Folklore also assures us that it is very unlucky to pluck twigs or foliage from blackthorn today. The tree - famous for its sloe fruits - is guarded by a species-specific member of the fairy tribe called the Lunantishee, and they are particularly vigilant today. They will do their will-o-the-wisp best to waylay and lead astray anyone who tries to approach a blackthorn, and will bring mishap to a person who succeeds in harvesting the tree on Old May Day. They appear to look a little more kindly on September's sloe harvest.

12th - Old May Day - LET THERE BE CHEESE

Pre-empting the summer solstice, weatherlore gloats about the onset of abundant daylight on Old May Day:

> *To the 12th of July from the 12th of May*
> *All is day.*

On the 12th of May, curds and whey... the 12th is also the traditional start of the cheese-making season. And what finer county in which to observe the ancient craft? With its Sage Derby, Stilton, Buxton Blue and Dovedale, Derbyshire is the cheese capital of Britain, as a visit to the famous factory cheese shop in Hartington will verify.

13th - LEAD TO MURDER - MAGPIE MINE

The lead miners of Wirksworth used to hold their May Day celebrations on this date (the day after Old May Day). They decorated the ravaged hillsides with greenery and held a day-long holiday of singing and dancing, feasting on beef, pudding and ale.

From the records it appears that the lead miners of Magpie Mine near Sheldon had too much on their plate to bother with May festivities. Today Magpie is a tourist attraction, being perhaps the finest surviving example of a lead mine in the country. It was first worked in 1740; but after the initial bonanza, with several hundred tons of metal per annum, there followed years of dispute, murder and mayhem. Fights broke out between the Magpie miners and those from Maypitt Mine, as both teams were working the same lead seam.

In 1833, after a few skirmishes and stalemate court cases, the Magpie men tried to smoke out the opposition by lighting an underground fire. Three men were well and truly kippered, and they failed to survive the ordeal. The ensuing court case failed to pin blame for the lead poisoning on any one man, as a result of which the widows of the three murdered Maypitt miners placed a curse on Magpie Mine. This Widow's Curse is said to have led to the site's closure in 1835, by which time it was riddled with ghosts.

Undeterred by its ill-omened past, Cornish miner-engineer John Taylor re-opened Magpie Mine in 1839. He improved the machinery, updated working practices, and managed to keep out of the courts. He continued to pump the flood-prone mine with mixed success; but in 1873 the much-needed drainage sough was excavated. The sough is a 2km channel from the mine to the River Wye near Ashford, and it took eight years to complete.

Production continued, but there were a number of closures and restarts in the 20th century, and Magpie closed for the last time as a working mine in 1954. It was back in the news in the 1960s, however, when a huge volume of water suddenly exploded from the sough. The channel had become blocked, water had built up behind the blockage and the resulting pressure resulted in a temporary water feature of volcanic proportions, washing away a large chunk of the hillside in the flood.

14th - STAB AND DELIVER - THE DERBY WAGON

Modern complaints about the quality of passenger and delivery services are easily silenced by a glance back to yesteryear. The Derby Waggon set out on this day in 1734 with far more to worry about than the present day post van or commuter. Highwaymen were a genuine and ever-present danger:

'This is to give notice that the Derby Waggon begins on Tuesday the 14th May 1734, sets out from the White Hart Inn at Derby every Tuesday morning and comes to the White Hart Inn in Friday Street, London on Saturday following and goes out every Monday morning at Ten o'clock... Performed (if God permit) by Thomas and Henry Partridge. N.B. They will not be accountable for any Money, Plate, Jewels, Watches, Rings or Writings (i.e. deeds, leases, etc) packed in Boxes, Parcels etc if lost.'

One record for 1741 states how two 'footpads' apprehended the Waggon on Finchley Common: *'They took from the Waggoner about 7/- who making a stout Resistance they stabbed him in three places in the back, each about two inches deep and cut the Sinews of his neck so that his Head lay on his Shoulder: after which the Villains made off: Some Higglers soon after passing that Way took up the Waggoner and carried him to Finchley but his Life is Despaired of.'*

In 1764 a faster version on steel springs, advertised itself in a splash of hyperbole as the Flying Machine. It could do the same Derby to London journey in two days. Not that this would have left the footpads behind - any Highwayman knows that you can do London to York in a single day.

15th - SOW DIRTY - MAY SUPERSTITIONS

Along with the three days on either side, May 15th is said to be the best time of year for sowing. Mid-month is also the best time to harvest wild garlic (ramsons). Folklore advises against washing and bathing during May - this and the wild garlic make a potentially formidable combination. The unclean approach is extended to the bedroom too:

> *You must not wash your blankets in May*
> *Or else you'll wash your soul away.*

23rd - CLOSET TALK - DERBY WORKHOUSE

Prior to the Welfare State, the unemployed poor, orphaned, elderly, disabled, sick and disturbed were all shovelled into the Workhouse. The alternative was a life begging on the streets; and it is doubtful which of the two provided the healthier option.

Some Workhouses gained relatively good reputations, but many would have suffered the various plagues of sickness, lack of hygiene, and swarms of invertebrate parasites. On this day in 1840 the governor of Derby Workhouse in his report noted:

'the Water Closets in the probationary are very much out of order somewhere, and the stench is becoming very unpleasant.'

This followed a similar complaint a year earlier, when he had made a plea to deaf ears: *'If something is not done with the Water Closets &c I fear we shall have a Fever in the House as the Summer advances.'*

Later in the year the governor suggested that, due to the high number of broken chamber pots, it would be 'better and an economy' to replace them in the rooms with communal buckets. (See also May 8th)

23rd - FIRING BLANKS - ROBERT CRYER OF GLOSSOP

Robert Cryer, Vicar of Glossop, died on this day in 1574. He had conducted a funeral nine days before, during which he came down with a fever contracted from a sick parishioner he had visited earlier. Cryer was locally renowned for his fondness of preaching in bursts of spontaneous blank verse. Some of these eccentric outpourings survive:

> *'Ill fated man why should'st thou take such care*
> *To lengthen out thy life's short Calendar:*
> *When every spectacle thou lookest upon*
> *Presents and acts thy execution*
> *Each droupeing season and each flower doth crye,*
> *'See how I fade and in the dust do lie'...*

24th - ONE FOR SORROW, TWO FOR DISSECTION

You think modern bird twitchers are odd? In 1951 the following record was placed in the Derbyshire Archaeological Journal:

'May 24th. Time 15-30 BST. Place: near Milton. Weather: sunny and hot after heavy rain. A Magpie's nest containing 5 young about 6 days old was found in an Alder tree.'

So far so good. However, it continues: *'The birds were killed and their gizzards opened immediately. The gizzards were estimated to be 100% full.'*

You would be forgiven for not being in the least bit interested; but this is what the murderous twitchers came up with:

40% unidentified animal material, 25% adult beetles, 10% Lepidoptera (butterflies and moths to you and me), 10% stones, and 5% each of spiders, beetle carval and unidentified plant material.

25th - St Aldhelm's Day - ASH SHREW! - BLESS YOU

7th century Bishop St Aldhelm, whose feast day this is, is associated with ash trees. He once planted his ash staff in the ground and it took root and bloomed. Since then ash has been known as Bishop's Tree and its curative powers have been attributed to Aldhelm; although the various superstitions surrounding ash have a pagan Saxon origin.

Locally the tree is commemorated in the place names Ashover, Ashton, Ashford, Ashbourne, Ashleyhay, Monyash, Borrowash and the former village of Ashopton, demolished to make way for Ladybower Reservoir.

It was once believed that ash could cure rickets and hernias; although each tree could only effect one cure in its lifetime. Saplings were split down the middle and children were passed naked through the cleft for healing purposes. The tree was then sealed up, and if the child survived the ordeal, its ailment would pass. If not, bad luck.

To cure animals, a shrew was sealed into a hole in an ash, a ritual which turned the wood into a livestock heal-all. Such wood can also protect a house from malign magic. This was largely a hair-of-the-dog type magic, as shrews were thought to blight livestock in the first place.

A vegan alternative is to place a horseshoe at the roots of an ash, oak or elm. You can also cure toothache by sitting under the tree and cutting your toenails.

28th - HITTING THE LOW NOTES

On this day in 1845 the prehistoric barrow Taylor's Low near Wetton was opened. In charge of operations was the amazing Thomas Bateman, the one man Time Team of his day. Following in the footsteps of his father William, who had excavated 11 barrows during his lifetime, Thomas took the archaeological race up several gears. Between 1843 and 1860 he managed to dig his way into an impressive 212 barrows.

Bateman's practices have since raised a few eyebrows. His recorded data is considerably sparser than a modern scientist would demand, and the dig-and-raid approach to archaeology is anathema nowadays. Bateman, however, was an enthusiastic pioneer, and his collection of 'Celtic' plunder was said to be second to none in the country.

Maligned as he might be today, Bateman was a popular local figure in his own brief lifetime (he was only 39 when he died). The opening of Taylor's Low was used as the frontispiece illustration to a contemporary, anonymous poem called *Barrow Digging* by 'a Barrow Knight'. The light-hearted verse manages to capture the man's enthusiasm and charisma:

> *And all exclaimed, their grog whilst swigging,*
> *There's naught on earth like barrow digging.*

Some of the lines do commend Thomas to posterity, however:

> *Then carefully replace the soil*
> *Nor for a moment stand, till*
> *The Lowe, by scientific toil,*
> *Is robed in its green mantle.*

Bateman also placed a lead marker in each of his digs, inscribed with his name, to tell future diggers that the site had been excavated previously. A forgiving soul by nature, posterity finds it hard not to forgive in turn; and his own writings serve as an apt epitaph for the man himself:

'...the [deductions of] *older archaeologists... were not infrequently erroneous. This, however, was a consequence more attributable to the uncertain nature of the study, then in its infancy, than to any defect of judgement or intelligence in the men themselves, whose mistakes we should treat with lenity.'*

29th - Oak Apple Day - ROYAL PUB CRAWL

Known far and wide as Oak Apple Day, in Castleton this is Garland Day. After riding on horseback around the ancient village boundary in Stuart costume, a Garland King dons a large beehive-shaped frame covered in flowers and greenery and parades on horseback with his female consort between the village's six pubs. Young girls in white dance throughout to the inexorable Garland Tune, played by the Castleton Silver Band.

At the end of his ordeal the King is relieved of his mobile hedge and the frame is hoisted onto the church tower, which has been decorated with greenery the day before. The event is rounded off with maypole dancing and a short ceremony at the war memorial, upon which the topmost part of the garland - the 'Queen' - is reverently placed.

Of course, everyone wants a music-and-greenery festival like this to be ancient. There are plenty of clues pointing obscurely back through the mists of time; but on the surface Garland Day, like all other Oak Apple Day observances, marks the return of Charles II to England and its throne after the short-lived Commonwealth.

The ceremony itself has changed over the last 100 years; and although the central role of the church may excite folklorists at first glance, it appears that the tower decorations were more to do with the bell-ringers, who received their annual 'bonus' from a whip-round on the 29th. The earliest record of some kind of ceremony in Castleton is from 1749 when a churchwarden recorded: *'Paid for an iron rod to hang ye singers garland - £0. 0s.8d'*.

None of which alters the fact that this is one of the country's most picturesque ancient ceremonies. Note, though, that if the 29th falls on a Sunday, Garland Day shifts to the 28th.

THE GARLAND KING

MAY SPECIAL DAYS AND BANK HOLIDAYS

Bank Holiday Weekend - WHIT'S END

Once upon a time there was Whitsun, a moveable holiday falling seven Sundays after Easter (see below). Its modern successor is the Late Spring Bank Holiday, and one or two old Whit customs still linger here.

The colourful and robust well-dressing, maypole dancing and tossing the sheaf competition at Endon is one set of events which has survived the move intact; although Endon is over the border in Staffordshire, so I am forbidden from going into any more detail. In Derbyshire there are well dressing events this weekend at Brackenfield, Wirksworth, Monyash and Middleton-by-Youlgrave.

Morris dancing is a traditional Whitsun spectacle, and you will be hard pressed to avoid a display or two over the weekend. There are many Morris teams in the county these days, the most ancient being Winster Morris.

One of the local tunes, *The Winster Processional,* is very similar to *The Castleton Garland Tune,* which is itself almost the same as *The Cornish Furry Tune* or *The Floral Dance.* It has been speculated that the Cornish tin miners who came to Derbyshire to work the lead seams brought the tune with them.

The Bamford Sheepdog Trials take place on Bank Holiday Monday. It is not an ancient festival - it was established in 1943 to raise funds for local men in the armed forces. It is, however, rooted in one of the oldest triumvirates in human labour - man, dog and flock. As the Trials' motto says:

There is no good flock without a good shepherd
And there is no good shepherd without a good dog.

ASCENSION DAY - THE WELL DRESSED FESTIVAL

Ascension Day, or Holy Thursday, is the Thursday after Rogation Sunday, the fifth Sunday after Easter. Beating the Bounds was a traditional Rogationtide custom, a communal reassertion of parish boundaries stemming from a time when such matters were constantly disputed and challenged. Boundaries would often be marked with a cross or stone, but most often it was a tree.

Gospel Elm in the parish of Church Broughton is an example of such a tree. The priest and congregation would process to the boundary tree and read the Gospel under its branches. The custom survived the Reformation, and saw a revival in several places in the 19th century. Gospin Knowl near North Wingfield is a corruption of Gospel Knowl (hill); likewise the Gospel Stone, a boundary marker for the Hathersage parish (formerly one of three such markers, it would appear from early references).

When a large chunk of the Hathersage estate was sold by William Fitzherbert and his son Basil, these outgoing Lords of the manor rode the bounds on August 7th 1656, prior to bowing out. It probably had nothing to do with nostalgia, and was merely a way of reasserting the legal bounds of the land mentioned in the deeds of sale.

Tissington, the accepted home of the modern well-dressing tradition, sets up its spectacular displays at this time of year. Before World War I the custom was a very neighbourly affair, with an open house policy throughout the village after the church

service, and a general holiday for all concerned. Local legend says that in 1615 there was a national drought, with just three showers of rain between March 25th and August 4th. Tissington's waters, however, never failed, and the festival originated as a thanksgiving. A good story - but records suggest a well-dressing ceremony here as early as 1350.

Apocryphal as the legend may be, any other guess about the origin of Derbyshire well-dressing is pure conjecture, tempting though the mists-of-

TISSINGTON WELL DRESSING

time pagan red herrings are. Records of Roman practices, involving the building of altars over springs and the offering of sacrifices, give lingering hope to the pre-Christian wishful thinkers.

The one thing the county's various well dressings have in common is sheer artistry. Nail-studded frames are covered with a mixture of clay, salt and water, and this is the canvas upon which the selected scene is 'painted'. Outlines are made using alder cones or dried beans in a process known as black knobbing. Colour is given to the picture via floral and vegetable material, although some villages allow wool and hair too. The completed tableaux are then taken to a water source, whether existing, former or imaginary.

The degree of pomp and ceremony depends on the location. Tissington is still the must-see example, from the dunking of the dressing frames in the village pond, to the finished work and subsequent blessing. The county currently boasts more than 75 well-dressings, brightening up the year from early May through to early September.

WHITSUN - BETTER LATE THAN NEVER

Whitsun was formerly one of the major feasts of the year. The name comes from 'White Sunday', and is thought to be a reference to white baptismal robes.

You would be forgiven for thinking that its various traditions of fairs, feasts and Morris dancing have fallen into disuse, but the truth is that the festival has been hijacked by the Late Spring Bank Holiday in May. This is far less moveable than Whitsun, which is the seventh Sunday after Easter.

Henry Kirke, in his article *The Ancient History of Chapel-en-le-Frith*, published in *The Reliquary* in July 1868, writes of an obsolete custom:

*'On Whit Monday they have a curious custom in this parish of providing every little child with a bottle, in which liquorice or Spanish juice is put and then hung round its neck by a st*ring. The children march to the wells and fill the bottles with water, which they then proceed to shake and suck at for the rest of the day. On this account the holy season is known amongst the juveniles as Bottle Day.' (See Easter Sunday).

It was the tradition to wear new clothes on Whit Sunday. In the Peak District it was said that birds would, otherwise, do what birds do from a great height, spoiling any old clothes with their droppings.

TRINITY SUNDAY - HARD TO BEAR

On the Saturday before Trinity Sunday (the one after Whitsun), Ashford-in-the-Water dresses its three wells. The well-dressing here was revived in 1930 after a lapse of many years. It used to be the centrepiece of the robust village Wakes, a week of sport and play that included a bear baiting, until that 'sport' was abolished by law in 1832. The permanent bear-tethering ring was fixed to a stone in the middle of the main road. When no dogs were available the bear was 'attacked' by men with wheelbarrows. The bear, apparently, would jump onto the barrow given half a chance - and if you had to abandon the barrow to the animal's possession you had to buy a gallon of ale as penalty.

The Thursday after Trinity is the feast of Corpus Christi. It is commemorated in an ancient piece of music, The Corpus Christi Carol, and the most celebrated version, Down In Yon Forest, was collected here in Derbyshire by the great Ralph Vaughan Williams (see December 25th).

WINSTER MARKET HALL

JUNE

1st - St Wistan's Day - HAIR-RAISING MARTYR

St Wistan, whose feast is today, is the patron of Repton. The town was the chief centre for Mercian Christianity in the early years of the church, and its Abbey was known as the Westminster Abbey of the North, due to its wealth of interred saints and royalty.

Wistan was a Mercian prince who objected when his cousin Berhtric announced that he was going to marry Wistan's mother Elfleda, the Mercian Queen. The cousin settled the dispute by burying an axe in Wistan's head, AD 850. This was somewhere in modern Leicestershire, and where his blood fell saintly supernatural hair sprouts every June 1st. The fact that no-one knows exactly where the murder spot is makes the annual miracle hard to disprove.

2nd - COURT JESTERNE - TEMPLE NORMANTON

On June 4th, 1467, at a Court session in Temple Normanton, it was heard how, on the 2nd, labourer Geoffrey Lee of Williamthorpe had attacked Robert Colley, the chaplain, with a jesterne (a coat of chain-mail). The assault left Colley with 15 wounds to the body and head, 'so that by many of the same he would have died if he had not had attention.'

We don't get to hear the outcome of this fracas, so we don't know what the penalty was for clobbering someone with a jesterne in the 15th century.

4th - FOUNT OF KNOWLEDGE: LLEWELLYNN JEWITT - WINSTER

Llewellynn Jewitt, Derbyshire historian, illustrator and long-time editor of a treasure-trove periodical called The Reliquary, died on June 4th 1886. He founded The Reliquary in 1860 and was its editor until the died. The journal was a celebration of 'legendary, biographical and historical relics', in Jewitt's own words: snippets concerning local history, archaeology, quirks and eccentricities. It was, thankfully, a far fuller and more inclusive concept than his first publication, A Handbook of British Coins; but the schoolboyish desire to collect, label and file remained his driving force.

Originally from Kimberworth near Rotherham, Jewitt gravitated via London, Oxfordshire and Plymouth to Derby. The original reason for this was to enable his ailing wife to recover in her 'native air' of Derbyshire. Llewellynn became involved at once with the city's museum, and launched the Derby Telegraph, the county's first cheap newspaper (1d weekly). He then moved to Winster Hall, and was involved in dozens of publications, from a history of the Volunteer Rifle Corps; to The Cross in Nature and Art with a thousand of his own engravings; to the more whimsical and indigestible

Florence Nightingale: A Tribute in Verse. He also collected a volume of ballads and songs of Derbyshire, pre-empting the later English folk song collectors.

Winster itself was in Llewellynn Jewitt's debt - it was due to his initial efforts that the village gained eight public fountains, saving villagers a three mile hike for fresh water. As his official obituary in The Reliquary of 1887 put it: 'The moral, social and sanitary effects of a plentiful supply of pure water cannot be over-estimated. The town was gaily decorated for the occasion of the inaugural ceremony. Flags waved from every house, and garlands were suspended at different intervals along the streets. The bells of the Parish Church rang a merry peal...' The pumps themselves were decorated with evergreen - a spontaneous outburst of well dressing.

When his wife died on March 4th 1886, Llewellynn never recovered, describing himself as 'lonely, desolate and sad'. On his deathbed in 1886 he claimed to have seen her ghost several times, and recorded on June 3rd that his wife was keeping vigil until his time came. She wished to take a walk with him, he said, and was now sitting patiently until he was ready to depart.

4th - THE RISE AND FALL OF THE BLESSED VIRGIN - BREADSALL

In 1914 church arsonists wreaked havoc in 23 Derbyshire churches, destroying five of them. Some commentators blamed suffragettes for the arson, but the jury is still out on it. The Rev Charles Cox (Llewellynn Jewitt's successor at The Reliquary) wrote in The Derbyshire Archaeological Journal that this vandalism was 'mad wickedness warring against god', and 'worthy of the Kaiser's hordes' - reflecting the country's concerns at that moment in time.

On June 4th 1914 All Saints at Breadsall was gutted by one of these fires. Amidst his righteous ire, Cox finds a positive note by celebrating the survival of a concealed Pieta (a statue of the Virgin with the dead Christ across her lap) which was undamaged by the fire. It was re-erected as a symbol of this minor triumph, only to fall off the wall face-first, with much disfigurement, a short time later. Breadsall was clearly getting mixed messages from the Divine.

7th - ALL HAIL ARMAGEDDON - CHAPEL-EN-LE-FRITH

Dr Clegg, Minister, Physician and diary-keeper of Chapel-en-le-Frith, made a vivid record of a particularly violent summer storm on this day in 1711:

'...flashes of lightning... succeeded by violent gusts of wind and rushing whirlwinds. When the cloud broke, with a prodigious noise, and fell in one of the most terrible tempests that was ever known in these parts, the stones that fell were many of them eight or nine inches about, and some larger. They were of bluish colour, and resembled pieces of solid ice, very irregular and extreme hard. These, being driven by a violent wind, accompanied by continuall flashes of fire from ye

W.N.W., did abundance of damage to ye houses, oxen, timber, and mowing grass which was within the compass and course it took, which was about 3 miles in breadth... ducks, geese, hares, pigeons, etc., were killed in multitudes; trees stripped of their bark, some torn up and others broke, which afforded a dismal prospect after. This was a dreadful day, and many thought the dissolution of things was at hand.'

9th - JUSTICE: MISSING IN ACTION - PENTRICH

On this day, in 1817, the Pentrich Rebellion broke out. Workers objecting to low pay, unemployment and lack of representation rose up and began a brief, fruitless protest, having planned their armed march in Pentrich's White Horse public house.

The prime movers of the Rebellion had contacted discontented parties across the county's various borders and beyond prior to the uprising; but to no avail. The army disbanded the men in mid-march, and they were all arrested and charged with insurrection. Most of the ring-leaders were transported, after being persuaded that a plea of guilty would save their lives. Some, on account of their ages, were allowed to go free. The low pay and disillusion remained.

11th - St Barnabas' Day - WOLFMEN - GLAPWELL CHARTERS

In 1176 the aptly titled John the Wolfhunter and Thomas son of Thomas Foljamb kept the wolf from the door on several acres in Peak Forest. The land was theirs to work as they saw fit, and the bailiffs demanded no rent on condition that the men planted wolf traps in March and September. In addition they had to hunt down the cubs on June 11th, St Barnabas' Day, the traditional date for carrying out this bloody exercise. Wolfhunter and Foljamb's tenancy agreement stipulated that they should not hunt the cubs with bows and arrows but with a hatchet, a spear, a knife in the belt, a mastiff, and a lad to carry the traps.

St Barnabas' was also Lamb Day, the time for handing over lamb tithes according to the Mediaeval feudal system (sometimes on the 12th or 14th). The

booty did not go to the local church directly,
however - Monyash parish records reveal
that sheep farmers in this region paid
their tithes to the Dean and Chapter
of Lichfield.   According to the
Glapwell Charters, in the 13th
century this lamb tithe would
have been a week premature, as
the traditional date for parting
the lambs from the ewes was June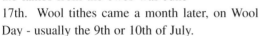
17th. Wool tithes came a month later, on Wool
Day - usually the 9th or 10th of July.

The Glapwell Charters are a collection of around 250 legalise documents, dating
from 1206 TO 1685, purchased for posterity by Derbyshire County Council in 1951,
and printed in the *Derbyshire Archaeological Journal* in two supplements over the
years 1956/7. The bulk of the material relates to Glapwell, where the documents were
kept by the Woolhouse and Hallowes families, residents at Glapwell Hall since the
late 15th century.

The earliest charter is between Nicholas de Verdun and 'Robert son of William',
whereby Robert receives Nicholas' sister Agnes in 'free marriage', along with 105
shillings and a pound of pepper. The latest is the intriguing entry for 1685 (86 years
after the penultimate entry), by which Thomas Hardwicke gives Thomas Woolehouse
of Glapwell *'the sum of nine pounds which is for the use and upon Account of Mistress
Mary Fisher of London'*. This, and a 1481 entry, are the only ones fully in English.
The bulk is in Latin, with a mixture of the two for some of the later entries.

12th - A SEVERE BLOW TO THE APPETITE - OVER HADDON

Martha Taylor of Over Haddon stopped eating in 1667, aged 18. It has been speculated
that the self-imposed starvation was brought on by a severe blow on the back received
some years before; although a modern reader must inevitably speculate that it
represents an early recorded case of anorexia nervosa.

There were a number of odd symptoms associated with Martha's condition,
including sensory difficulties, vomiting and an effusion of blood from the eyes. This
excited curiosity rather than emergency medical care; and to ensure that the fast was
genuine the neighbouring townships and the Duke of Devonshire set a watch on
Martha. Between 40 and 60 women kept an eye on her by rota 24 hours a day. The last
pamphlet detailing the 'miracle' - for these fasts were thought to be religious statements
rather than a comment on the quality of the local produce - was published in 1669.

Martha had taken little more than a drop of milk or wine and a few raisins for much of her fast; but at some point after 1669 she seems to have recovered. She died in June 1684 and was buried on the 12th. It is not known for sure whether this case was a hoax or whether it was an illness with several incidents of remission. Whatever the truth, it seems more than likely that the region's other celebrated faster, the hoaxer Ann Moore of Tutbury (see May 4th) was inspired by the pamphlets about Martha.

16th - HERON AID - NORBURY MANOR

In 1603 Richard Topcliffe, a much hated henchman of the Mafia-like Privy Council, put aside his hard-man image and wrote an ingratiating letter to Derbyshire-based bigwig, the Earl of Shrewsbury, at Norbury Manor.

Usually a man of double-dealing and intrigue, Topcliffe clearly tried to curry favour by rustling up some choice seasonal cuts for the nobleman's larder. He sent the Earl four pieces of venison, from *'the best stagge that I have seen (of a wilde deere) in whittson weeke'*, Whitsun being a traditional time for culling deer on an industrial scale. Warming to his culinary theme, our hitman-turned-chef went on about *'yonge heronsawes out of the nestes which well Baked is excellent meate coulde or hotte & better than roasted.'*

Strictly speaking 'young heronsawes' is tautological, as 'heronsawe' is the name for a young heron. The bird featured in most 16th and 17th century cookery books, and was always described as a delicacy. It was also claimed that when heronsawes fly above the clouds, rain is on the way. This weatherlore still applies, to both young and more long-in-the-beak herons.

17th - BAD DEBT, GOOD BEER

Ralph of Wessington had fallen into massive debt in 1252. To evade the moneylenders he gave over all his lands, goods and wealth to Darley Abbey. This was in order to cheat the lenders of their prey, as the law dictated that they could not seize monastic property. Although now officially bankrupt and without a single worldly possession, canny Ralph had struck a deal whereby the Abbey henceforth provided him and his family with all necessary comforts. According to this deal, he and his wife Matilda received 14 white loaves and 14 gallons of 'good beer' per week, along with hand outs of meat and fish according to the season (including a lamb or two, perhaps, see June 11th).

For their two servants they received 28 'service loaves' and seven gallons of 'second beer' weekly. In addition they were allowed 'good lodging', and fuel for their fires. Ralph also had recourse to one of the Abbey's horses whenever he needed it. Each year he was allowed clothes, or the cloth to make them, for himself and Matilda, plus shoes twice a year and yearly linen for underclothes and bedding. Their two sons were provided for, too.

There is something apposite in those references to beer, as the little that remains of Darley Abbey today is a flourishing pub in the suburbs of Derby.

Saturday before the third Monday in June - FLASH TEA POT

The Flash Teapot Parade takes place on this day in windswept Flash, which is said to be the highest village in England, 1,500ft above sea-level between Buxton and Leek. The parade is a simple affair organised by the local Friendly Society, the Flash Loyal Union. A brass band leads the paraders to Flash Bar on the A53, which just happens to be the site of the Travellers' Rest pub. The sense of being slap-dab in the middle-of-nowhere is ironic, as Flash is almost in three places at once, being close to the Three Shires Head boundary between Derbyshire, Staffordshire and Cheshire.

The Parade gets its name from the tea which is consumed at the private meal afterwards, and from the teapots which used to be given out as prizes for the person who won the gurning competition.

Gurning, for non-initiates, involves pulling a hideous face, usually through a horse collar or 'braffin'. As with all such contests, there is a story at Flash which maintains that one year's outright winner complained on the grounds that he hadn't yet started gurning.

21st - STONED CIRCLES - SUMMER SOLSTICE

The Summer Solstice, give a cosmological tweak or two, tends to fall on this day, and you would be hard-pressed to dissuade the average latter-day Druid or neo-pagan from going about their spiritual nostalgia today. Sites such as Arbor Low and the Nine Ladies on Stanton Moor suddenly defy the uncertainty and mystery that does, in reality, shroud them, and become simplified temples for whatever tickles your post-Enlightenment fancy.

In reality, everyone knows that the best sight on the Summer Solstice in this part of the world is the famous Double Sunset in Leek. From the churchyard of St Edward's, looking out to the hills, the sun appears to set twice in the space of a minute; but as that's over in Staffordshire I shouldn't go on about it too much.

23rd - St John's Eve - MIXED HERBS

This is another good day for spotting fairies. In fact this day is second only to

Hallowe'en for supernatural encounters of all kinds. To offset the worst of this, country folk used to make a herb garland from herbs gathered at first light today. (Most would collect some dew while they were there, too, as St John's Eve dew has curative properties). The garlands were hung on doors to offset evil influence, or burnt on bonfires at sunset.

The most efficacious of all the herbs is St John's Wort, a yellow flower linked to ancient sun-god worship (St John being the saint roped in to challenge the original pagan patrons of Midsummer). Other good choices include ivy, plantain, corn marigold, vervain, orpine and yarrow. It should be borne in mind that picking wild flowers is actually illegal these days. If you don't want to discourage fairies, the Stocking Field at Calver was once renowned as one of the best fairy haunts in the county. At dusk they engage in a circle dance.

24th - St John's Day - WAKE THE MORRIS - CARNIVALS

Tideswell was given a fair charter in 1250, for the eve and day of the feast of St John the Baptist (23rd and 24th), patron of the local church. It was moved to August 29th, the Beheading of St John the Baptist, in 1391, but is now back where it began, thanks to the magnetic pull of the village's Well Dressing and Wakes Week. On the main Carnival Day Morris Men dance the traditional *Tideswell Processional.*

Several other villages hold their Wakes and well-dressing over this week too, including nearby Litton, which is famous for its tug-o-war competition. Other well-dressings include Youlgrave, Kniveton, Chelmorton, Hope and that epitome of ancient rural pastime, Derby. There are several more during June, including bouts at Bakewell, Elmton, Whaley Bridge, Tintwistle and Old Whittington at the end of the month.

Strangely devoid of a well-dressing, Winster Wakes are amongst the county's most celebrated, largely because they date from way back when and feature the renowned Winster Morris. (See May Bank Holiday Weekend). There are four known dances indigenous to Winster: *The Winster Processional, The Winster Gallop, The Winster Reel* and *The Blue Eyed Stranger.* All four will be on show during the Wakes, as will the Morris entourage of Fool, King and cross-dressing Queen.

Morris Men and spectators alike will be keeping their fingers and sticks crossed for fine weather. It will come as no consolation whatsoever to hear that, in weatherlore, St John's Eve rain presages a wet harvest to come.

Midsummer festivities at Chapel-en-le-Frith used to centre around a rushbearing ceremony. According to Churchwarden accounts it cost 15 shillings in 1734 - a sum which, these days, wouldn't even pay for half a pint of the hundreds consumed as part of the celebrations. The fact is that although the church-centred concept of rushbearing sounds like a peaceful occasion, in Chapel it was a day of feasting and excess. In 1745 Dr Clegg, local physician and Minister, noted that there was a riot, and that two people in the Royal Oak pub had their arms broken in the melee - probably fighting to see who could spend the 15 shillings first.

24th - ROSE AND ROSE OF RENTS - SUDBURY

According to the eccentric *Rhymed Chronicle* of John Harestaffe (see December 1st), in his will of 1600 John Vernon of Sudbury Hall left to one William Fernihough a small portion of land with a peculiar, though not unique in the annals of arcane custom, rent to be paid on this day:

> *To William Fernihough then did he give*
> *To have and holde as long as he should live*
> *Of meadowe ground one acre, and to pay*
> *A rose for rent, on St John Baptist's day.*

A similar arrangement is made for another servant, Walter Peerson:

> *...An Acre which within Brode meadowe lyes,*
> *For one and twentie yeares or otherwyse*
> *Until ye full terme of three lyves were spent,*
> *Yealdinge a red rose yearlie for his rent.*

This would appear to be a lease for whichever proved the shortest: 21 years, or the life of Peerson and his heirs. (See Tithes, April).

26th - GRAVE NEWS - CHAPEL-EN-LE-FRITH

The well-weathered quill of diarist Dr Clegg scribbled down details of an earthquake on this day in 1748: '*In the evening after I returned home, about 10 minutes past five, we felt a shock of earthquake, which startled us all, and sadly terrified some young women with us. It shook the whole town of Chapel-en-le-Frith, and all the ground about it, and all about a mile about us, but, blessed be God, no harm was done.*'

You might think that a bit of an anti-climax; but the following incident soon makes amends. The quake was followed by another great storm which caused mass flooding, just as impressive as the one mentioned for June 7th.

Preacher extraordinaire John Wesley was doing his thing in the neighbourhood at the time of the storm, and recorded the truly horrifying scene: *'There fell rain for three hours, which caused such a flood as has not been seen here before. The rocks were loosed from the mountains; the fields covered with large stones; water-mills washed away; trees torn up by the roots; two women swept from their own doors and drowned. Hayfield churchyard all torn up; dead bodies swept out of their graves. When the flood subsided, they were found in several places - some hanging in the trees, some in meadows, some partly eaten by dogs.'*

29th - St Peter and St Paul's Day - NO RUSH, NO SWEAT - RUSHBEARING

A flower was often used on the old runestick almanacs to mark this day, being the symbol of Peter and Paul, on whose day medicinal flowers should be gathered. This is probably the reason why June 29th was the most popular day nationally for the tradition of rushbearing (June 24th & August 12th). Local sources of the vegetation can be deduced from the Derbyshire place-names Rushap and Rushley, along with several local field names. Poor drainage made rushes very common and the use of fresh rushes in churches was a necessity, being the only means of keeping the unsavoury floors dry.

In 1881 a correspondent of *The Derbyshire Archaeological Journal* wrote: *'The custom has only died out within the last fifty years in many parts of England.'* As key places where it lingered he mentioned Chapel-en-le-Frith and Glossop, and Whitwell where hay was used instead of rushes. This hay came from a meadow called the Church Close, and was strewn with due ceremony on St John's Eve (23rd). In Glossop the rushes were piled high on a rush cart, the centre of a day of dancing and celebrations not dissimilar to the surviving (or, rather, revived) rushbearing festival at Saddleworth in Lancashire, held during August.

The custom was not without its downside, however. Erasmus, in writing of the curse of 'sweating sickness' in early 16th century England, wrote:

'Englishmen never build their chambers in such a way as to admit ventilation... The floors are in general laid with a white clay, and are covered with rushes, occasionally removed, but so imperfectly that the bottom layer is left undisturbed, sometimes for twenty years, harbouring expectorations, vomitings, the leakage of dogs and men, ale-droppings, scraps of fish, and other abominations not fit to be mentioned. Whenever the weather changes a vapour is exhaled, which I consider very detrimental to health... I am confident the island would be much better if the use of rushes were abandoned.'

Erasmus was Professor of Greek at Cambridge, and a celebrated writer. He had turned his thoughts to the sweating sickness - an infectious disease similar to the plague - after a nasty outbreak in London during 1507.

ASHBOURNE MARKET PLACE

JULY

1st - HAILING PIGEON EGGS

Tempests in July are said ruin the year's harvest. Abraham Jones of South Wingfield could certainly vouch for that fact. Jones was another of the county's many diary keepers and chroniclers, writing in the first half of the 19th century. He often wrote in verse, on the most mundane of matters; but he also recorded an impressive tempest which mugged South Wingfield on this day in 1826.

July always inflicts a thunderstorm or two on England, but not many are as impressive as the one Jones recorded. Describing the 'mournful visitation' he mentions that the corn crop was indeed ruined, and that *'vast quantities of little birds were killed. Many of the hailstones which fell were as large as pigeons' eggs, and some were larger than geese eggs; and notwithstanding the excessive heat of the sun, they lay upon the ground four days, before they melted.'*

Abraham Jones and the residents of South Wingfield were thankful that the following weather rhyme only applies to ordinary precipitation:

> *If the first of July be rainy weather,*
> *It will rain more or less for four weeks together.*

If the 1st is a Friday, it's a fait accompli, as weatherlore tells us *'The first Friday in July is always wet'*.

1st - BLAGRAVE TAKES HIS CUT - BARTON BLOUNT

A Civil War skirmish took place at Ashe, a small village between Sutton and Etwall in the south of the county, on this day in 1645. A contingent of the Parliamentarian garrison based at Barton Blount Hall was involved, from the commandeered building that was able to feed and water 700 cavalry.

The best insights we have into the skirmish and the general conditions at Barton Blount come from physician George Blagrave, who kept a record of the work he carried out mending the wounded men after the Ashe battle - or, more accurately, a record of the expenses incurred.

By the standards of the time, Blagrave was expensive: *'At the fight near Ashe on Tuesday the first of July John Cox I cut in his hand and a very soare wound in his arm - £1 0s 0d'*. His most expensive listed case, at £1 10s 0d, was the unfortunate *'John Bullock of Capt Barton's, a very sore cut in the forepart of his head which caused a piece of his skull the breadth of a half crowne peace to be taken forth, alsoe a very sore cut over his hand.'* Tending ten wounded Cavalier prisoners costs £5 according to Blagrave's bill.

The village of Barton Blount was abandoned after the Civil War, and the Hall fell into decay. The only action it has seen since 1645 was when local farmers corralled their cattle in a depression in the park grounds to avoid them being spotted by the omnivorous advancing forces of the Stuart Pretender's rebellion in 1745, en route from Ashbourne to Derby. It is also reported that Zeppelins flew over the abandoned Hall during their raid on Derby in 1915.

George Blagrave died in 1653. He received an effusive epitaph in All Hallows Church, Derby, on account of his many skills as surgeon, sexton, songsmith, poet and turner.

2nd - WEATHERLORE IN TRANSLATION - ST SWITHUN

July 2nd is the feast day of St Swithun - not, however, the one upon which a downpour indicates rain for the next 40 days. That takes place on July 15th - the feast of the translation of Swithun's bones to Winchester Cathedral in AD 971.

Today's St Swithun's, which is also the feast of The Visitation of the Virgin Mary, was often marked on runestick almanacs with the symbol of two crossed branches. Interestingly, given Swithun's more famous link with weatherlore, it is said that however the weather turns out on this day, so it will remain until July 29th.

First Sunday in July - HOLY LOVE-IN - ALPORT CASTLES

This is the day for the Alport Castles Love Feast, in the middle of nowhere above Alport Valley off the A57 Snake Pass. A few makeshift benches and some straw on the floor are the meagre comforts offered to the congregation at this annual religious meeting.

It was instigated as a result of the Dissenter witch-hunt in the 17th century, which drove zealous and unintimidated worshippers to isolated locations such as Alport Castles. Because the wine and wafers of a normal church service are not allowed in the unconsecrated farm building, spring water and fruitcake have been substituted, the water being passed around in a two-handled Loving Cup. Some families claim to have been attending the event since its humble beginnings.

Going back to the origins of the Love Feast, it began in 1662 after a religious purge afterwards known as Black Bartholomew Day, when 46 clergymen were cast from office for refusing to accept the religious dogmas of the day and leaning instead towards the movement that would become known as Methodism. The black-listed 'psalm-singing rascals' met in secret at Alport Castles to hold services and receive alms. Sentries high up on the moors warned of any approaching trouble. John Wesley revived the meetings in the 18th century; and although the original Love Feast hayloft and cow byre have now been swallowed up by an adventure training centre, the sense of being in the middle of nowhere survives. The event is still resolutely religious, and the lack of piano gives an ideal excuse for no-holds barred Methodist hymns and vocal decoration.

1st weekend in July - THIS VILLAGE IS BUGGED - BUXTON FESTIVAL AND WELL DRESSINGS

There are a number of well-dressings at this time of year, including ones at Hathersage, Chapel-en-le-Frith, Tansley, Dore and Buxworth. Dore's celebrations only date back to 1959, but have become a symbol of the village's Derbyshire roots since it was swallowed whole by Sheffield in the boundary changes of 1974.

Buxworth was formerly spelled 'Bugsworth', a fact which polarised views throughout the 20th century. In the 1920s the change to the 'x' spelling occurred, resulting in the local doggeral:

Bugsworth bells are ringing so joyfully and kind,
For Bugsworth now is Buxworth, ineffably refined.

The fact that the change was made for reasons of snobbery - 'bux' was reckoned to sound a bit posher than 'bugs' - resulted in a counter-snobbery backlash at the end of the century, when there was a very vocal campaign to put the 'Bug' back into the village name.

Meanwhile, the first weekend in July sees the beginning of the greatest three weeks in the county's more famous 'Bux', with the Buxton Festival and Festival Fringe turning the town into a small bit of Edinburgh here in the Peak District. The famous St Anne's Well is dressed on the Sunday, with a fair and carnival the following weekend. (July 24th for more on St Anne's).

4th - I PROTEST - KEDLESTON

The Protestation Oath was mouthed by the House of Commons in 1641, to affirm a number of central commitments which everyone in a position of power or influence was obliged to make. The Oath was copied into the registers of many Parishes, including Kedleston, where 36 parishioners, led by minister Walter Taylor, signed it on this day in 1641. Of the signatories, 22 were unable to write, leaving their mark (a cross) instead.

The meatiest points in the Oath were: To defend lawfully, with life, power and estate, within the Realm, the *'true reformed Protestant religion... agaynst all popery and popish Innovations'*. In addition, everyone had to show allegiance to the Monarch and Parliament, and to support the rights and liberties of the King's subjects. They also promised to bring punishment to anyone who opposed any of these ends *'either by force, Practice Counsels, Plotts, Conspiracyes or otherwise'*. Signatories also vowed to *'preserve the Union and peace betweene the 3 kingdoms of England, Scotland & Irland.'*

Irony found all this irresistible, and the hot air about peace and allegiance to monarchs dissipated during the following year, which saw the outbreak of full-blown civil war, resulting in the execution of Charles I.

5th - FLOORED BY SICKNESS - DARLEY DALE

'Sweating sickness' was a common, and usually fatal, ailment in the 16th century. As we have seen, writer and philosopher Erasmus implicated bad floor hygiene as the main breeder of the problem (see June 29th).

In the Registers of Darley Dale, a 1551 entry says, with a matter-of-factness typical of these records: *'Nine persons were buried on the 5th of Julye till the 10th, which died of ye sweatinge sicknenes.'*

9th - ARGUMENT DISSOLVES - MONASTERIES

At the beginning of the Dissolution of the Monasteries, in 1535, several houses were exempted from suppression. Dale Abbey, Repton Priory and St Mary's in Derby all survived the first wave; but it was clear from the start that the stay of execution was only temporary. The main weapons of the men sent to investigate Abbey practices were charges of idolatry - the over-use of idols and relics - and accusations of sexual activity. At Dale, for example, Abbot John Staunton was eventually accused of affairs with two women, one of whom was married; and a monk was said to have had sexual relations with five women.

On July 9th 1537, an employee of the brutal mastermind of the Dissolution, Thomas Cromwell, reported to his master how a hermit in St Thomas' Chapel, Chesterfield, had spoken 'after a rage fashion' before a host of holy men and commissioners. The hermit concluded the outburst with words which capture the whole episode in a nutshell: *'...and that the pope, now called the Bishop of Rome, was deprived of his authority because he would not consent to the King's marriage...*

if a man will pluck down or tear the King's arms he shall be hanged, drawn and quartered. What shall he do then that doth pluck down churches and images, being but a mortal man as we be?'

In 1539 the last of the monastic houses of Derbyshire were dissolved.

10th - WEATHER RAINS SUPREME - WOOL DAY

The spectre of rain and its ongoing consequences casts a long shadow over the month of July. St Swithun is only half the story (see July 2nd). On this day, five days before the famous Saint's threat of a forty-day deluge, weatherlore tells us: If it rains on the 10th of July, it will rain for seven weeks - that's nine more days than Swithun's threat. This was also Wool Day, the time for handing over wool tithes (see June 11th).

16th - PORK CONDITION - BASLOW

Robert Watson had a novel way of attempting to bring home the bacon. The Court Rolls of Baslow record that in the 16th year of Richard II's reign (1393) *'Robert Watson sued Nicholas del Hay because his dog had worried a pig at his house to the damage of 5 shillings. The accused denied the charge. In mercy.'*

The same day's Roll has the enigmatic entry: *'Adam le Partrykhunter has a ruinous house.'* The name Partrykhunter, i.e. 'partridge-hunter', was probably a nickname for a poacher. A ruinous house was, clearly, a criminal offence. Delineating a moment in time according to the year of the King's reign rather than the familiar AD 'Year of Our Lord' number was popular in Mediaeval records.

16th - THE HOLE TRUTH - BLACK HILL

William Wood was returning to Eyam after selling cloth in Manchester on this day in 1823. Meeting three apparently affable locals, he made the mistake of stopping for a swift pint at a roadside inn in Chapel-en-le-Frith. The three men had not failed to notice Wood's bulging pockets. Later, confronting the man on the eastern slopes of Black Hill, the three demanded his money. When he refused to comply, the muggers resorted to hammering William Wood's head into the ground with a rock.

This gory detail is important, as the hole made by Wood's head became barren, which was deemed to be a sign of supernatural discontent. The truth is that a monument detailing the death (the facts having been dragged from one of the apprehended murderers) turned the site into a minor tourist attraction, and many feet and hands rummaging at the spot would have kept the place barren with or without uncanny intervention.

In the 1850s the hole was approximately two feet long and four inches deep. Local lore insisted that no grass could grow there, and any soil, turf or rocks piled into the hollow were scattered on the nearby road when no-one was looking. It was certainly a very unusual way of conducting a haunting.

The so-called Murder Stone on the minor road between Whaley Bridge and Disley in Cheshire can still be seen. Two of the murderers were later caught and hanged; the third was never apprehended.

Third Sunday in July - THE DERBYSHIRE HIGHLANDS - ASHBOURNE

English Highland Games may be rarer than a sheep's pluck haggis at a Vegetarian dinner party; but the Ashbourne Highland Gathering, set in the rolling hills of Derbyshire, is the genuine article.

Founded in 1985, the Gathering incorporates the All England Highland Games Championship, and boasts a full programme of entertainment, characterised by massed pipe bands, kilts and caber-tossing. The side-shows range from falconry displays to dancing JCBs, while the town's eateries are briefly transformed into Burns' Night theme pubs.

Third weekend in July - THE WICKER MAN'S LAST STAND - STAINSBY

Stainsby Folk Festival attracts upwards of 2,000 people on the third weekend of July. Once a year this sleepy village, nestled between Chesterfield and the M1, is transformed into an all-singing, all-dancing insomniac. The Festival features a low key but well chosen selection of bands from the folk and acoustic circuit, plus the usual array of ethnic stalls, fast food vendors and pub-style sessions from musicians great and small.

Each year a giant wicker effigy is constructed and torched on site; although the increasingly jittery wolves of the insurance industry may eventually stamp out this fine tradition. The music will doubtless continue.

19th - UNHOLY WATER - DERBY

More July rain - the following was recorded in the Churchwardens' Account Book of the Church of St Werburgh in Derby:

'July 19 1673. Being Sabbath Day at night theare was a great ffloud the water was two ffoot high in the middle alley it weare mesured so that it came into cheasts & wett all the writings such a ffloud were not known in our agge before. Cloves to sweeten the church after ye flood - £0 0s 2d.'

The true role of burning incense in High churches becomes clear in this context. Cloves and other spices - juniper, cinnamon, frankincense, even charcoal and tobacco - were burnt to disinfect and sweeten the air.

There was another flood in St Werburgh's in 1687 during November, at a clean-up cost of £0 1s 4d. On July 15th 1691 an outlay of 2d managed to block the North door, in an effort to hold back future floods. In 1696 the blocked door did its business, keeping that year's floodwater at bay; but there was another church-breaching deluge in 1715, after which 9d was spent *'for levelling ye North Alley after ye flood.'*

20th - VERY MOORISH TORNADO - WHALEY BRIDGE

A tornado ravaged the countryside from Macclesfield Forest to Whaley Bridge via Taxal and beyond on July 20th 1662. Local reportage was at hand to capture yet another example of the violent weather so common to high summer, this particular record *'given by Mr Hurst, minister of Taxal, who had it from an eye witness'*:

'In the afternoon, in the Forest of Maxfield, there arose a great pillar of smoke, in height like a steeple, and judged twenty yards broad, which, making a most hideous noise, went along the ground six or seven miles, levelling all the way; it threw down fences and stone walls, and carried the stones a great distance from their places, but happening on moorish ground not inhabited, it did less hurt. The terrible noise it made so frightened the cattle, that they ran away, and were thereby preserved; it passed over a corn field, and laid it as low with the ground as if it had been trodden down by feet; it went through a wood, and turned up above an hundred trees by the roots; coming into a field full of cocks of hay, ready to be carried in, it swept all away, so that scarce a handful of it could afterwards be found, only it left a great tree in the middle of the field, which it had brought from some other place. From the Forest of Maxfield it went up by a town called Taxal, and thence to Whalley Bridge, where, and nowhere else, it overthrew an house or two, yet the people not much hurt, but the timber was carried away nobody knew whither. From thence it went up the hills into Derbyshire, and so vanished.'

The 20th is famous for its generally bad weather. It is the feast day of St Margaret, and her symbol on the runestick almanacs (April 14th) was usually a pail, symbolic of the bucketfuls of rain expected today.

21st - BRIGHT SPARK LIGHTS CHURCH - ASHBOURNE

It's all well and good churches being a light in the darkness; but solving the practical problems of darkness inside the building itself was not always as easy as the flick of a switch. Ashbourne church records for 1559 have the following note concerning the issue of *'Endowments for Perpetual Lights in the Church of Ashburne'*:

'Queen Elizabeth, on 21st July, in the 1st year of her reign, granted to George Howard, Knight, inter alia one parcel of meadow lying in the parish of Ashburne, called Lampholme meadow, in the tenure of John Knifton, given for the maintenance of a lamp in the Parish Church of Ashburne.'

In other words, via this simple but effective remedy all profits from the meadow would go towards keeping the lights switched on in the holy edifice.

24th - The Vigil of St James - WHERE THERE'S A WILL THERE'S A WAKE JOHN FITZHERBERT OF NORBURY

The death of John Fitzherbert, 12th Lord of Norbury, occurred on this day, the Vigil of St James, in 1531. He asked to be buried in Norbury Church *'under the newe made arche benethe the Steple or els where God shall otherwyse dispose it'*. His detailed will gives a fascinating insight into how a man of wealth made detailed plans for his soul, his memorial and his family.

Fitzherbert left 13 pounds of wax, to be burnt as tapers continuously around his coffin for the first seven days of his wake. Every mourner at the funeral was to be given a farthing loaf and a penny of silver, with the same to be delivered to the priests and clergy seven days later, and the same again to the poor. Lord John was eager that prayers should be said at his tomb on a regular basis after the funeral and wake, especially during Lent. To this end he instructed that all householders on his lands were to send a representative during this time, to keep vigil, for which inconvenience they would be paid two farthing white loaves and two herrings. If herrings were not available, a piece of silver was to be given instead; although further research is needed to ascertain how many herrings you could buy for a piece of silver. On Easter Eve the same vigilant householders were to receive two farthing loaves and a piece of beef from half a roasted fat ox, specially barbecued for the occasion.

Fitzherbert also paid for masses and requiems to be said for him in a number of holy edifices, including Coventry and Lichfield Cathedrals and Darley Abbey. Doling out money even further afield, the generous Lord gave 10 pennies to every

Austin and Carthusian monastery in the land (just five years before the Dissolution of the Monasteries began), and paid for the building of a bridge in Rochester.

Closer to home, he gave six young ewes to each of his servants at Norbury Manor and elsewhere, with the stipulation that all the staff were to be kept in their positions for at least 40 days on their old wages. Letting bygones be bygones - as if there's much choice after death - Fitzherbert also gave 20 shillings to redeem poor debtors.

In the bosom of the family, Lord John went into great detail doling out goods to his two daughters and the rest of his kin, declaring that his brother Henry was to inherit the estate, and that a certain Anne Welles and her husband John, who were trying to claim that Anne was an illegitimate daughter of Fitzherbert's, were to get absolutely nothing.

Fitzherbert's monument can be seen in Norbury Church, one of the finest village churches in the county.

24th - GARLICK & OTHER CATHOLIC TASTES - PADLEY MARTYRS

Nicholas Garlick and Robert Ludlam were Catholic priests from Derbyshire who had trained in France. Not exactly a hanging offence these days, but back in the late 16th century they were risking their lives by preaching in the county. Catholicism had been outlawed, and any priest trained on the continent was not even supposed to set foot on English soil. However, protected by local landowner and Catholic recusant John Fitzherbert (see previous entry for his father's pro-Catholic will), things seemed relatively safe.

What no-one had banked on was the greed of Thomas, heir to the Fitzherbert estates at Padley near Grindleford. To pre-empt his inheritance Thomas alerted the thought-police to the illegal presence of the priests. The Rev Charles Cox wrote in *The Derbyshire Archaeological Journal* in 1885:

'Nicholas Garlick and Robert Ludlam... were taken to Derby Gaol. On July 25, 1588, Garlick and Ludlam (together with a third priest seized elsewhere) were hanged, drawn, and quartered, and their heads and quarters fixed on poles in prominent places about the county towns, solely for the crimes of being Roman priests.'

John Fitzherbert joined his brother Thomas who had been in prison for reasons of faith since 1561. Both died in gaol.

On the same day in 1681 one George Busby was arrested for the same popish crime - by that time £100 was the reward for apprehending any practitioner of the Roman faith. Not much had changed in a hundred years - and Busby was sentenced to be hanged, drawn and quartered.

A commemoration of the Padley Martyrs takes place annually on the Thursday nearest July 20th. Hundreds attend the procession, which goes from Grindleford Station via Padley Mill to the ruins of Padley Hall.

26th - St Anne's Day - ALL WELL AND GOOD

ST ANNE'S WELL

St Anne is best known in Derbyshire as the patroness of Buxton's famous well. The saint herself is apocryphal, a hastily sketched Mother of The Blessed Virgin, roped in to fight the good fight against the pagans. The delights of Buxton's waters were probably old news when the Romans arrived here and founded the town of Aquae Arnemetiae - *'the waters of Arnemetia'*. Arnemetia was a local water deity, and the 'Arne' bit of the name is, via assonance, the sole reason for 'Anne' being superimposed here in the Christian era.

A 1709 travelogue by an unknown author records the mineral waters in Buxton as being *'extreamly warm... much courted in the summer by ye Nobility and Gentry, having medicinal vertue in em good for Stomach nerves, sinews and the whole body.'* Sounds like a good cue for a fully-fledged spa town and tourist industry... On a more poetic note, Thomas Hobbes in his *De Mirabilis Pecci* describes the well as:

> *This fountain sacred to St Anna's name,*
> *A stream from thence both hot and cold does rise*
> *In which a Pharmaceutic vertue lies.*
> *It gives the aged Paralyte reliefe,*
> *And nourishes the nerves grown cold and stiff.*
> *It doth the sick unto their health restore,*
> *And makes the same to need the crutch no more.*

Or, in the words of Charles Cotton in his *Wonders of the Peak*:

> *Hither the sick, the lame and the Barren come,*
> *And hence go healthful, Sound and fruitful home.*

During the Spa boom in the 18th century, Buxton was developed as a resort with all manner of drinking and immersion cures on offer. The old bath houses survive in a number of guises, and the main well still pumps out a regular 200,000 gallons of ancient water daily at a constant, tepid 28C.

27th - EXPOSING THE MEAT - DERBY

Derby's last Royal Charter contained good news for mayors who long to carry a white staff and mace; but nothing but bad news for meaty foreigners:

'1682. July 27. Warrant for a new charter to the borough of Derby with a privilege to the mayor to carry a white staff and to have the mace before him on all public occasions, and a provision that butchers that are foreigners shall not expose their meat before 12 in the market on the market day being the usual time of ringing the market bell, and that at sunset they pack up.'

28th - HARD TO STOMACH - BAKEWELL

Bakewell diarist and geologist White Watson noted on this day in 1799 that he had seen - and he sketched it for posterity - *'a newt which Mr Joseph Carrington, Surgeon of Bakewell, said he had brought from a Lady's stomach in Buxton in June 1799.'* The sketch is vague - a ragged, slimy animal with a cigar-like body. What we don't find out, I'm afraid, is how the newt managed to find this unlikely resting place.

29th - St Olaf's Day - COLD RESPONSE TO OLAF'S MOON

It is said that if the full moon falls on this day, a severe winter will follow. Olaf was an 11th century king of Norway, and is now that country's patron saint. He was revered in those parts of England subject to the Danelaw in the 9th and 10th centuries, including Derbyshire.

Last Sunday in July - THE CIRCLE GAME - BURBAGE

This is the day for the Clipping Service (or Clypping) at Burbage, which is now part of Buxton. Revived in 1975, the ceremony involves the symbolic 'clipping', or embracing, of the local church by the hand-holding congregation. There are hymns, prayers, and, hopefully, enough people to form the full circle.

If you're getting all excited thinking that this sounds like a pagan revival, you'll be devastated to learn that the first ceremony took place in 1851. (September 8th for more Clipping).

BUXTON CRESCENT

AUGUST

'Before Lammas' - MERCIA UPON US

Lammas falls on August 1st; and before you mutter 'so what?', over to our Anglo-Saxon Chronicle correspondent in Derby, standing with warrior Queen Athelflæd...

'Before Lammas, Athelflæd, the 'Lady of the Mercians' won the borough called Derby with God's help, together with all the region which it controls. Four of her thanes who were dear to her were slain there within the gates.'

The Queen secured Leicestershire the following year, consolidating her hold on most of the Midlands.

1st - Lammastide - LOAFING AROUND

Lammastide is an ancient harvest festival. The name Lammas comes from the Anglo-Saxon *hlaf-mas*, meaning 'loaf-mass', the first bread of the new crop being so important both physically and symbolically that it gained its very own church Mass. Lammas was also a key time for trading sheep - an important industry in this part of the world. So, serendipitously, Lammas can be interpreted as 'lamb-mass', as long as you don't mind having irate etymologists hammering on your door.

In addition, Lammas is the feast of Lugh (pronounced loo), Celtic god of autumn sun, fun and harvesting. To underline this, the Celtic name for the festival is Lughnasadh. It has always been a time for fairs, festivals and general merriment. In Derbyshire the tradition continues in several places - Bonsall Carnival lasts for a week, commencing on the last Saturday in July, and the massive Bakewell Show, dating back to 1848, takes place over two days in Lammas week.

Casting less of a shadow over history, but thoroughly in the Lammas celebratory spirit, the Buxton Gilbert and Sullivan Festival kicks off at the end of July and lasts throughout Lammas week. There are also innumerable small-scale fairs, car boot sales and general summer festivities throughout the region. Quite how many of those involved are celebrating Lugh or Lammas is a different matter.

First Saturday in August - CHICKEN COUP - BONSALL

The chicken-fixated Barley Mow pub in Bonsall hosts the World Hen Racing Championships on the first Saturday of August, one of the highlights of the week-long Bonsall Carnival. Around 30 hens compete for the title each year, and although the prizes may be chicken feed, the glory of victory should not be underestimated. After his triumph with plucky Ginger Rogers in 2003, Phil Addis became the world's most successful hen-racer, Ginger being his third victorious bird.

Spectators and entrants are encouraged, and there is live music and real ale to calm your sporting nerves. In recent years a new mechanical chicken category has widened the field even further.

1st-7th - BRADWELL WELL DRESSING -
A CORNER OF DERBYSHIRE THAT IS FOREVER CORNWALL

Bradwell's well-dressing takes place on the first Sunday in the month. Admire the intricate flower-pictures at the two wells, and pity the poor Hope Valley gardener, for a local saying in these parts is 'no garden is sacred.' In other words, at this time of year that fine old tradition of flower filching runs rampant. Having said that, many of the blooms on display are hydrangeas, and the bulk of these traditionally comes from - of all the unlikely places - Trelissick Garden in Cornwall.

3rd - FIRE AND WATER - CROMFORD & RICHARD ARKWRIGHT

Derbyshire industrial giant Sir Richard Arkwright, one of the founding fathers of the Industrial Revolution, died on this day in 1792. Cromford Mill was the first and most important of his cotton mills, and it was here that he developed the water frame mechanical spinning process that revolutionised the manufacture of cloth and brought him fame and fortune.

The first Cromford mill was built in 1771, with a second mill and extensions added down the years, along with buildings on various new sites. Only the original Cromford mill survives today - the second one burnt down in 1890, 22 years after the Arkwright mill at Bakewell had met the same fate.

After Arkwright's death there were further revolutions in the industry, and in the 1830s steam-powered mills in Lancashire, and at the nearby Masson Mill upstream from Cromford, made the water frame machines obsolete.

In 1979 the Arkwright Society acquired Cromford Mill, spending millions on its restoration. It is now a popular tourist attraction.

8th - GETTING THE ARBOR LOW-DOWN

Arbor Low, near Monyash, was subject to trowels and modern archaeological inquiry on this day in 1901, by archaeologists from the Anthropological Section of the

British Association. The chief aim was ascertain the age of the slightly crestfallen monument, and to make an informed guess concerning its purpose and usage. Arbor Low is the foremost henge monument in Derbyshire, with a high bank and ditch enclosing a ring of fallen megaliths. The 1901 dig set out to bulk out the pure guesswork of previous commentators with a bit of science. It was not even known at that point whether the megaliths had ever stood upright.

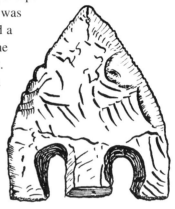

After the dig, however, everything - and this is perhaps as it should be with ancient monuments - was inconclusive. No metal was found, which suggested a late Neolithic dating, a hypothesis backed up by the discovery of late Neolithic barbed flint arrow heads. Sadly, little else was unearthed which could verify a construction date.

The 1901 casebook, then, was far from closed. Just ten years later a member of the Derbyshire Archaeological and Natural History Society argued that Arbor Low was simply a corral for cattle or sheep. Similar arguments have been put forward to account for other henge monuments. It is not quite as exciting as the notion of astronomical clocks or druidical rituals, but at least it maintains the impenetrable sense of megalithic mystery.

Whenever you visit Arbor Low - whether it's grim and brooding under a steel sky, frosted by the breath of winter or awash with summer grass and neo-pagans - you depart afterwards with the wonder of something so large and vital in the landscape, and yet as inscrutable as a divine poker game.

10th - St Bertram's Day, St Lawrence's Day -
ANGLO-IRISH RELATIONS FALTER: WOLF IMPLICATED

Bertram, aka Bettelin,was an Anglo-Saxon prince who eloped with an Irish princess. Tragically, the princess went into labour in the middle of a forest, and, having failed to pack towels and hot water, the panicking Bertram ran for help. In his absence the princess and her child were devoured by wolves, convincing the luckless Bertram to take up the Hermit option.

It is a vivid tale, but like many stories of the early saints it has to be filed in the Tall Tales section. Bertram's actual life and deeds have, like King Alfred's cake recipe, passed into Dark Age obscurity.

Bertram's grave was said to be near the old well beside the church. The well itself was renowned for its ability to disappear at will. Whatever, the church at Ilam still houses the saint's tomb-shrine, and postcards are provided for enlisting the Saint's intervention - most unusual in an Anglican church. Bertram will do his utmost to address your stated ailments; although if his success in assisting the Irish princess is anything to go by, it might be best not to get your hopes up too much.

This is also St Lawrence's Day. Weatherlore attempts to assure you that if the day is clear, the winter will be severe. If it's misty, the year will be damp.

11th - Old Lammas Eve - SHEEP IN A LATHER - BRETTON

Old Lammas Eve is another traditional day for sheep fairs. Sheep have always been abundant in the Peak District area of the county. William Camden in his 1586 *Britannia* mentions that *'...though rough and craggy in some places, (the Peak) has also grassy hills and vales, which feed an abundance of cattle and great flocks of sheep.'*

Bretton in particular used to be famous for its woolly inhabitants, and its August 11th sheep festival was one of the country's rowdiest. The highlight was the sheep race, which started at the Barrel Inn. This event was odd on a number of accounts. Firstly, only one sheep took place at any given time. Secondly, only the most aggressive rams were chosen for the racing. Thirdly, to make it a clean contest, the rams were covered in soap. The race was between Bretton men, who attempted to catch the animals in order to win prizes. Free trips to the hospital, presumably.

The Week of the 12th
PUMP IT UP - BARLOW WELL DRESSING

Barlow dresses its three wells at this time. The ceremony in its present form began in 1840, when the well was graced with a pump and stone basin. It has not missed a year since. Only whole flower blooms are used in the well-dressings, and the pictures usually take the form of a triptych. The timing of the ceremony is linked to St Lawrence's Day on the 10th, Lawrence, the only saint to be martyred by getting barbecued on a gridiron, being the patron of the village's Norman church.

Between 9th & 15th
DEFEATED BY THE OLD QUARRY - WHITWELL

Whitwell folk had always visited High Hill quarry on the Sunday nearest the 12th in honour of St Lawrence, the village's patronal saint. In the 1870s this pilgrimage was formalised into an annual open-air service, with villagers perched precariously around the quarry in a thanksgiving for the founding of the church, which was thought to have been made from High Hill stone.

But in the 1980s it all started to go wrong. The symbolism was chipped away when someone pointed out that the church stone did not actually match up with the quarry stone; and then the local authorities donned their nanny-state boots and declared the outdoor congregation unsafe, with the paranoid equation: quarry + congregation + gravity = plummet to death. The thanksgiving service is still held, and the old *Ballad of Deacon Lawrence* is still sung, but it now takes place inside Whitwell church. Public Safety 1, Romance 0.

Between 12th & 18th - FOWL MOORS, FOUL FLOORS - FOREST CHAPEL

The Sunday after the 12th is the usual day for the Rushbearing ceremony at Forest Chapel in Macclesfield Forest. However, it often falls on any convenient Sunday near the 12th, at the discretion of the Earl of Derby, who comes here to shoot grouse on the so-called Glorious Twelfth.

Bunches of locally harvested rushes decorated with flowers are placed in the churchyard and around the pews and porch of the village church. The service begins inside (with a PA system for those outside), but it concludes in the churchyard against the impressive backdrop of the open hills and moors.

It is all an echo of the days when church floors were covered with fresh rushes to discourage damp, mice, and people who visit churches just to complain about the dirty floor. (June 29th for more on rushbearing).

13th - THE TURKEY AND THE NIGHTINGALE

One of Derbyshire's most celebrated residents, Florence Nightingale, died on this day in 1910, aged 90. For many years she lived at the picturesque Lea Holme near Cromford. The house is now an old people's home, and its Rhododendron Gardens are open to the public.

As every school child used to know, Florence was known as the Lady with the Lamp after her overhauling of the military hospital system during the Crimean War. Her efforts won her the Order of Merit, and a fund set up in her honour resulted in the founding of the first modern nursing school, St Thomas' Hospital in London.

Florence was born in the Italian city of that name. She was lucky - her unfortunate sister was born in Naples, and laboured under the ancient name for that city, Parthenope. The Nightingale first began to sing following a vision in 1837, when God informed her that she had a mission to fulfil. Only in 1854 did the calling

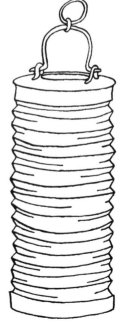

FLORENCE'S LANTERN

become clear, and Florence began her good work amongst the casualties of the Crimean War, in which Britain, France and Turkey were attempting to give as good as they got to the Russians.

15th - MUSICIANS' UNION: THE EARLY YEARS - TUTBURY CASTLE

In Mediaeval England anyone with a joke to tell, a song to sing or a bare bottom to flash joined the minstrelsy trade. However, the minstrel's reputation for shamelessness and excess earned him many enemies, which is why, in the 14th century, minstrel guilds were formed, to give the trade a respectable image and to look after members' interests.

Membership money financed an annual feast, presided over by an elected King of the Minstrels. One of the chief guilds was centred at Tutbury Castle, rebuilt in 1361 by John of Gaunt, whose lands straddled Derbyshire and Staffordshire. Only members of the Minstrel's Court of Tutbury were allowed to ply their trade in the two counties, a law which was backed up by the threat of fines. An early 17th century by-law warns non-members: *'no musician or minstrell shall hereafter use or exercise the said Arte or Science of Musicke within the said Counties for benefit or gaine.'*

The Tutbury King of the Minstrels was an important member of the community, and he presided over the Minstrel's annual knees-up on August 15th each year, the Feast of the Assumption of the Virgin Mary. The day was a celebration of the minstrelsy trade, with ornate speeches, a modest amount of guzzling, and a bout of bull-running.

The poor bull had its horn tips removed, its ears and tail cut off, its body smeared with soap, and its nose blown full of ground pepper so that it was in a mood to disembowel all participants. Everyone except the town's exalted Minstrels would then retire, and the bull-runners endeavoured to cut some skin from the enraged bull before it managed to run across the border into Derbyshire. The one who succeeded in this task was awarded with the title King of Music's Bull. Only then was the bull taken to the High Street to be tethered and baited with dogs. The 'KOMB' disposed of the body as he saw fit afterwards.

The day's highly dubious sport then degenerated into a career through the street with cudgels, aimed at bull and fellow man alike. The tradition was allegedly introduced to Tutbury in the mid-14th century by John of Gaunt, who had witnessed bull sports in Spain.

In the 1370s the Feast was described as an occasion promoting *'jollity, peace, honesty, sweetness, gaiety and love'.* But by 1778, when the white wands which symbolised the King's office had been replaced with fighting cudgels, the event had degenerated into *'rancour, felonies and all manner of vice',* and the Minstrel's Feast's three-century long song was finally suppressed in that year.

24th - UNAPPEALING PEALING - CASTLETON

You would have thought Castleton had quite enough bell-ringing already. The church tower reverberated several times every Sunday, nightly from 29th September to Shrove Tuesday, and on various other special occasions besides.

However, Robert How, the Barmaster - a local lead mining magnate - clearly thought the village needed even more of the same. On his death, this day in 1866, he left money to pay for the annual Barmaster's Birthday peal. That's right - more bells.

24th - St Bartholomew's Day - BARTHOLOMEW'S FAIR

This day is the traditional beginning of the harvest season in this neck of the woods. Weatherlore says if it is a fine clear day, the outlook is tip top.

25th - THE BAKEWELL STEEPLE CHASE

On this day in 1825, Bakewell church lost its original steeple and gained a town of poets. Rebuilt twice in the 18th century (1709 and 1726), repaired in 1818 and assessed as safe in 1824, by 1825 the steeple's imminent collapse forced the demolition team to move in.

Local satire came to the fore, with printed doggerel including the scathing *'A Great Bargain',* which bewails the fact that the steeple's composite parts were being sold, apparently to line the Vicar's pockets. It concludes:

> *Be not afraid of being left i'th'lurch,*
> *We've no objections bargaining for the church -*
> *Buy th'church and steeple, rump and stump,*
> *You shall have the Vicar given in with th'lump.*

A pithy pro-Vicar reposte appeared 2 days later on the 27th:

> *They in contempt would have you hold*
> *A man whose worth's as sterling gold,*
> *While they together, rump and stump,*
> *Form out a base and sordid lump*
> *Of malevolence.*

In February the following year a more considered and flowery verse appeared, *'Lamentation for the Loss of the Beautiful Spire of Bakewell'*:

> *Ye lisping babes, rise, and bedew with your tears*
> *The broken remains of these antients of years;*
> *Record to posterity's latest son's son -*
> *The grace and the beauty of Bakewell are gone.*

The *Lamentation* does not lay the blame at anyone's door, and concludes:

> *And disgrace not your ancestors' great and good merit,*
> *But prove you possess yet some spark of their spirit:*
> *From her now ruined state let her instantly rise,*
> *With her spire, as before, pointing up to the skies.*

Unlike the dodgy verse the problems did not end here, for the entire church was crumbling. It was condemned by architects in 1829; and in 1830 the churchwarden stopped the church clock, fearing that its striking would cause the tower to collapse. It was, indeed, partly dismantled soon after.

But matters eventually took an upturn, and both tower and steeple were rebuilt in the 1840s, just as the *Lamentation* had urged. Many wonderful Norman and Anglo-Saxon stones were found during the restoration, and they can still be seen in the church's south porch.

The churchyard's fine 9th-century cross has born silent witness to all these ungodly dramas.

26th - SHOTTEN LUCK - SMALLEY

Lightning never strikes twice, but it sometimes strikes three times at once.

On this day in 1680 at Smalley, Thomas Holland and his two children Thomas and Catherine were, according to local records, *'shotten and kill'd with thunder and lightning'*. All three were buried in Smalley churchyard the following day, and a well near the old post office was afterwards known as Holland's Well in commemoration.

27th - HOT AIR FROM THE PULPIT - CRICH

His sermons may be forgotten, but the Vicar of Crich made his mark on posterity by delivering a stirring, eccentric farewell speech. When he retired on this day in 1837, he told his flock:

> *My sledge and hammer lie reclined,*
> *My bellows, too, have lost their wind,*
> *My fire's extinct, my forge decay'd,*
> *And in the dust my vice is laid;*
> *My coal is spent, my iron's gone,*
> *My nails are drove, my work is done;*
> *My fire-dried corpse lies here at rest*
> *And, smoke-like, sears up to the bless'd.*

> *If you expect anything more, you are deceived;*
> *for I shall only say, 'Friends, farewell, farewell!'*

Bank Holiday weekend, August - ARTS AND CRAFTS

The August Bank Holiday weekend is marked by all manner of events across the county, from fell walks and birdwatching trips to craft fairs and Arts festivals. Expect happy family queues at every major tourist attraction, and scenes in Buxton, Bakewell and Matlock more reminiscent of Regent Street in the week before Christmas than quiet Derbyshire market towns.

Of the weekend's long-established events, shoppers swear by the Bank Holiday markets at Chesterfield, Glossop and Buxton; there are various carnivals, including ones at Leek and Eyam; and those with an eye for sheep, country crafts and all things agricultural are well served, with Country Shows and Sheepdog Trials at Hope and Chatsworth.

Between 25th and 31st - FLEA OR FLEE - EYAM

The last Sunday in the month is Plague Sunday at Eyam, commemorating the decimating effects of the 1665-6 plague and the bravery of rector William Mompesson and his self-sacrificing flock.

A batch of flea-ridden London cloth brought bubonic plague to the village, the first victim being George Vicars, the tailor who received the material. The Reverend Mompesson took immediate action to seal the community, establishing a 'cordon sanitaire' around the village. This contained the disease, but resulted in more than two thirds of the Eyam population perishing. One of the victims was Mompesson's young wife Catherine.

An 1863 description of the events supplies the purple prose: *'Catherine fell by the touch of the purple-visaged pest, while utter extermination was the soul-sickening expectation of the remaining few.'* Before leaving Eyam in 1669, Mompesson had a tomb erected over Catherine. This can be seen in the churchyard, along with the village's magnificent Saxon cross.

Preceded by a street procession, the Plague Commemoration service takes place al fresco in the dale of Cucklett Church (aka Cucklett Delph or Cussy Dell) just outside the village. This is where Mompesson held his twice-weekly services for the 14 months during which the plague raged.

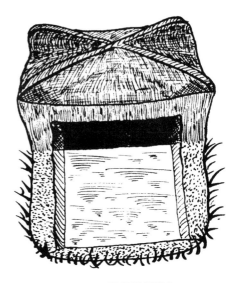

MOMPESSON'S WELL

It is worth underlining the fact that the ploy worked - every family in Eyam was touched by the disease, but it was successfully contained. You can still see several 'plague cottages', along with Mompesson's Well, where villagers left money to be disinfected by the pure spring water, in payment for goods brought in from the outside.

On a lighter note, during this same weekend Eyam dresses its wells, doing to the local flora what the plague did to the human population.

30th - ARCHITECT RUNS RAMPANT IN BUXTON

Buxton's Pavilion Gardens were opened to the public in 1871. The icing on the cake was the completion of the Pavilion buildings, designed as a miniature Crystal Palace, with a grand concert hall, opened by the Duke of Devonshire on this day in 1876.

It was the conclusion of a Duke-inspired Buxton architectural renaissance, the famous Crescent having been the first of the new buildings back in 1780, built as a scaled-down version of the Royal Crescent in Bath.

The former Royal Devonshire Hospital's huge unsupported dome was erected over the Duke's stables, and now smiles down upon the lucky inmates of Derby University.

31st - JUDGEMENT DAY SPOOKS HAYFIELD

The Last Trump sounded prematurely in Hayfield this day in 1754. A communal grave of flood victims rose up in front of several eye-witnesses at the ancient church of St Matthew. Looking understandably bedraggled, but clearly on a heavenly mission of some importance, they ascended into the sky in their hundreds, clad in gold and white. The witnesses were treated to a heavenly chorus, and the dearly departed left the air deliciously perfumed. John Wesley had been doing some recent preaching in the area - perhaps the corpses were liberated by his piety. Or perhaps they'd had enough of his grim sermons.

Hayfield Church itself, like many of the region's religious edifices, contains some interesting monuments. *Nottinghamshire and Derbyshire Notes and Queries*, in July 1896, reckoned the most noteworthy one belonged to Joseph Hague, described in his lifetime as one who *'wearied not in well-doing'* - a very satisfying epitaph to take with you into the afterlife.

Hague started his working life as a lowly pedlar, redefined himself as a successful merchant and ended his days as a wealthy man, thank you very much. He died at the age of 90 (*Notes and Queries* fails to give a year) - but one obituary described him ambitiously as 'nine score', which is 180. Plenty of time to rise from poor pedlar to rich merchant, then.

The bust surmounting Hague's monument was made by the sculptor Bacon, and used to live in the church at Glossop. During restoration work in that church the bust was placed for safety in the local lock-up, which was rarely used back then, thanks to the law-abiding townsfolk of Glossop. Unfortunately, this sober and orderly spree came to an end while Hague's bust was still chilling out. A drunk and disorderly local was locked in the mini-gaol by an unsuspecting constable, and this young man allegedly mistook the white marble head-and-shoulders for a truncated ghost. The bust suffered disfigurement during the ensuing, one-sided brawl, and the Hague family were so angered by this violent hangover that they had the monument removed to Hayfield.

Like all the best yarns, this one has a coda. Years later an elderly visitor to Hayfield was gazing at Hague's bust when the verger happened to mention the story. The stranger then confessed that he was that self-same, much-sobered drunk who had caused the damage. He claimed to have visited many countries in the intervening years but had always been weighed down by his guilt.

MATLOCK FROM HEIGHTS OF ABRAHAM

SEPTEMBER

1st - St Giles' Day - A FINE SAINT

This is St Giles' Day. His symbol on the runestick almanacs was a millstone - if the day was dry, weatherlore maintained that mills would lack water. In general, a fine September 1st leads to a prolonged spell of fine weather.

First Weekend September - JOKE WITH A TWIST - CHESTERFIELD WELL DRESSING

Wardlow dresses its wells this weekend, with the blessing on the Saturday afternoon. We are at the tail end of the well dressing season by now, and your only other chances of catching the tradition are over the Staffordshire border in Longnor on the second weekend, and at Hartington and Chesterfield mid-month.

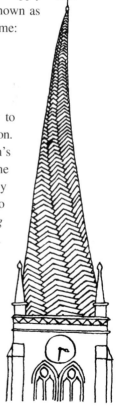

Dressing the wells is a form of thanksgiving for a good water supply. This is something they could do with at a certain boggy field known as Leechfield, or Leech Fend, near Little Baslow, as in the local rhyme:

> When Leech-field was a market town,
> Chesterfield was gorse and broom;
> Now Chesterfield's a market town,
> Leech-field a marsh is grown.

Leechfield was probably never a town, although its similarity to Lichfield can, if nothing else, afford a few lingering seconds of confusion.

Chesterfield is more famous for its 14th century church's crooked spire than its wells. There are several tales telling of the amazing structure's origins. Most of them involve the clumsy work of Satan; and one strand maintains that the spire turned to look when someone declared 'A Chesterfield virgin is getting married!' This probably passes as the earliest Essex Girl joke, 150 miles from home.

In reality, the spire's twist, which causes it to lean more than eight feet from the vertical, is due to the drying of unseasoned timbers and a split in one of the main support beams. The effect is accentuated by the herring-bone pattern of lead plates on the spire's eight flat sides.

The phenomenon has fascinated and baffled folk down the years. In the late 19th century the pages of Notes and Queries held a vigorous discussion featuring a faction who insisted that the Cathedral had been ingeniously planned this way.

2nd - GRINDING POVERTY - DERBYSHIRE FOOD RIOTS

Bread has always been a staple part of the diet. When grain prices have risen beyond the means of the poor, the result has been an inevitable marriage of famine and rioting. These so-called food-riots were common throughout the 18th century. Corn dealers and millers - who could fix their own fees and portions - were the prime targets for the crowd's anger.

On September 2nd 1756 the Derby Mercury reported extensive riots in Derby and Wirksworth: *'a great mob arose... and pulled down several Corn Mills in that neighbourhood.'* A week later the paper reported that mills in and around Derby had been attacked by *'a large number of Miners and other persons out of the Peak.'* It appears the acts of violence were very personal, aimed at specific millers and corn dealers.

Of the two, it was the millers who offended most. With the introduction of highly efficient grindstones, known as 'French stones', in the 18th century, they were able to mill much finer flour. With these stones anything could be ground down and passed off as wheat flour, according to the rioters. Millers were accused of grinding peas, beans and alabaster to bulk out their produce, and a certain Mr Evans, Miller of Darley, was said to have *'boasted that he could grind ten pounds of corn into twenty pounds of flour.'* Mills containing the French stones were popular targets for attack, and the property of the aforementioned Evans was certainly not spared.

3rd - WRIGHT ON - JOSEPH WRIGHT OF DERBY

Derbyshire's most famous painter, Joseph Wright, was born in Derby on this day in 1734. He was buried at St Alkmund's church, in the city, on September 1st 1797. The best place to admire his work is in the Derby Museum and Art Gallery, which has been wooing tourists since 1879.

During a stay in Rome, Wright painted his celebrated picture *The Captive*, using a hired beggar as his model. Upon its arrival in England the picture caused certain confusion at London's Custom House, due to the disreputable appearance of its subject. The eldest of the Commissioners commented:

'If any gentleman at this

Honourable Board chose to have his picture drawn, would not he put on a clean shirt, and have his wig powdered, and be clean shaven - answer me that? To be sure, he would. Now, it is here pretended that this fellow sat for his portrait, who had hardly a rag to cover his nakedness. Gentlemen, if he could have afforded to have paid for painting his picture, he could have afforded to buy himself a pair of breeches!'

Several paintings inspired by Wright's Italian tour depict Mount Vesuvius. One such piece was commissioned by an Irish Bishop, who later tried to knock down Wright's asking price by questioning the artist's skills. Viewing the work in progress, the Bishop suggested that Wright should in future avoid painting fire, for which he clearly had no aptitude. The accusation was versified by the poet William Hayley:

> *'Indeed, Mr Wright, you mistake or neglect*
> *The true tint of fire and it's proper effect,*
> *I wonder you think of employing your hand*
> *On a branch of your art that you don't understand.'*

Wright was justly famous for his wonderful depictions of fire: *'alone he rules his element of fire'*, wrote Hayley. So, not surprisingly, the painter was incensed. In the poem he replies:

> *'You black dilletante! Hence learn to your shame*
> *No mortal can give more expression to flame!*
> *If in flashes more brilliant your eyes wish to dwell,*
> *Your Lordship must go for your picture to Hell!....*
> *And the Devil, who often creates himself mirth*
> *By caricaturing odd beings from this earth*
> *Would find proper hints for his pencil to sketch*
> *In a mitre bestowed on so sordid a wretch.'*

Suffice to say, Wright refused to let the Bishop have the picture of Vesuvius, at any price.

4th - ON THE HUNT - EYAM

Joseph Hunt, Rector of Eyam, died in December 1709 in some notoriety. His fame stemmed from a drinking session in the Miner's Arms Inn following the baptism of the landlord Matthew Ferns' baby son. During the celebrations Hunt began flirting with the landlord's 18-year-old daughter Ann, and the drunken fun ended with the two undergoing a mock marriage ceremony.

The next morning's sobriety was particularly painful. Joseph Hunt was engaged to a Derby girl already; and the Bishop of Derby himself was soon on the case. Hunt, he insisted, must marry Ann Ferns of Eyam.

The proper ceremony was duly carried out on September 4th 1684; and lawsuits from the broken engagement pursued the Rector throughout his life. It is said that the vestry in Eyam church was built for the sole purpose of enabling Hunt to hide from his persecutors.

The full tale can be read in the Miner's Arms, which also claims to be *'one of the most haunted houses in the village, and has seen many strange events.'*

First week of September - FEELING A LITTLE SHEEPISH - LONGSHAW

The Longshaw Sheepdog Trials are held on the first Thursday, Friday and Saturday in the month. First mooted in 1896, the event's origins have a slight whiff of apocrypha about them. A group of shepherds were said to have met at the Fox House Inn to arrange a pigeon shoot on Totley Moor on March 24th 1898. Quite why there was to be such a long gap between the meeting and the event is unclear; even more bizarrely the shepherds then agreed that they knew little about the sport and didn't have enough guns to go through with the plan. In a blaze of inspiration, someone suggested holding a sheepdog trial instead.

March 24th 1898 responded to the meticulous, if convoluted, planning with a violent snowstorm. Undeterred, the shepherds held the event on the following day ...and this time they chose the Longshaw estate, not a million miles from the Fox House Inn.

The Trials are thriving now as never before, and can be enjoyed every year in the field opposite Longshaw Lodge off the Grindleford Road.

Sunday after 8th - CLIP ROUND THE EDIFICE

The bare details of the Church Clipping at Wirksworth, i.e. holding hands and dancing around a sacred site, sound pagan. The practice, however, could not be more genteel and Christian. Parishioners walk clockwise around Wirksworth church after the 10am Communion service, and then encircle it, holding hands and singing hymns. At least, they encircle it as far as they can - if numbers are down, only select bits of the edifice get to feel the full force of the loving embrace. There is usually a street procession afterwards.

The word 'clipping' comes from the Old English *clyppan*, meaning 'to embrace'. There is a similar ceremony at Burbage (the last Sunday in July).

10th - ASSIZE TOO BIG - TIDESWELL

A venison shortage in Westminster can lead to a corresponding venison shortage in Tideswell. Edward I had been hunting there in August 1275, and on this day an order was sent to Roger Lestrange, bailiff of the Peak *'to cause all the venison in the king's larder at Tydeswelle to be taken and carried to Westminster to be delivered to the keeper of the king's larder there'.* A long journey south under the summer sun would doubtless have guaranteed a somewhat gamey flavour.

Tideswell was in no position to complain, however, as it was apparently enjoying a spot of unlawful law-making. A 1276 entry in the records notes: *'Tudiswell have assize of bread and ale, but they know not by what authority'*, i.e. there had been no charter to hold an assize and feast in the first place. An 'assize' was a local court with set meeting times, tackling everything from felonies to the price of local produce. In its original Anglo-Norman sense the word means both 'a sitting' and 'a settlement', each definition highly appropriate to these gatherings.

10th - St Barloke's Feast Day
PATRON SAINT OF OBSCURITY - NORBURY

The feast of St Barloke celebrates an obscure saint, the original patron of the church at Norbury. Turning to the *Oxford Dictionary of Saints* for enlightenment, we are met with the words *'Nothing is known about him.'*

Some scholars think that he must be the same as St Barry (aka Barrog, Barruc or Barnic), a 6th century British anchorite buried on Barry Island. It must therefore be assumed that he was instrumental in bringing religion to this area; although whether in person or via a set of relics and some enthusiastic followers, we do not know.

It undermines the Barloke = Barry theory to discover that the latter's feast day is September 27th.

2nd Sunday in September - CONGREGATION OUSTS CHOIR - SALTERSFORD

Harvest festivals weigh down the nation's altars with tins of beans and sacks of spuds at this time of year. The open-air affair at the Jenkin Chapel in Saltersford is a notable example of the genre. It takes place in a particularly wild part of the Derbyshire uplands. The bleakness is not undermined by the simple austerity of the 1733 Chapel in which the festival takes place. For one thing, it is far too small to hold all the attendees, forcing the choir to sing to the gathered throng in the windswept graveyard. The chapel, meanwhile, is stuffed with more fresh produce than a Tesco theme park.

Harvest Thanksgivings such as this are relatively new institutions. The first one was held in Cornwall in 1843, and from then on they gradually ousted their rumbustious predecessors, the Harvest Homes. The latter were marked with feasting, drinking and music, celebrating the bringing in of the local grain crops, with all the usual rowdiness and excess.

13th - DROWN IN THE FLOOD - RIVER DERWENT

More heavy rain blights the region - according to the Darley Dale registers: *'1648, Sept. 13 - A male child of Robert Gregory, of ffrogatt; drowned, brought downe the River in the fflood.'* In folklore rivers are usually ambivalent forces of nature, and the Derwent was no exception. Usually a haunt of fly fishers and tourists in these parts, it was also a bringer of death and destruction, as this child tragically illustrates.

13th - THE WOLFISH HEIGHTS OF MATLOCK

The scenic limestone tops of Matlock Bath, all tourist trade and cable cars, would seem an unlikely place to commemorate the Battle of Quebec in 1759, in which the British army under General Wolfe defeated the French Host of general Montcalm, thus winning Canada for the British. The deciding battle was on Quebec's Heights of Abraham. A few years later, a Derbyshire man who had fought with Wolfe declared that the high bits of Matlock reminded him of the battle site. Since then the area has been known as the Heights of Abraham.

14th - Holy Cross Day - FITZHERBERT RAMS

Derbyshire's earliest farming book was Fitzherbert's *Boke of Husbandrye,* printed in 1523. Capturing the extant wisdom and lore of the time, it includes the instruction that for the common man *'it is tyme to put his rammes at the exaltation of the holy cross'.* Today is the feast of the celebration of The Cross upon which Christ died (the only surviving day dedicated to the Cross since the Roman Catholic church cancelled the feast of the Finding of the Cross in 1969). The injunction *'time to put his rams'* refers to the fact that sheep should be bred at this time of year.

Fitzherbert's *Boke* also makes notes about the variety of wheat grown in the Peak District: *'Peeke Wheate hath a red ear, ful of anis, thyn set, and oft times it is flyntered, that is to say, small corne, wrynklled and dryed, and wyll not make whyte breade, but it wyl growe upon colde ground.'* We get the impression that this last detail was, in Derbyshire, the key one.

Despite this promising wheat analysis, the common Derbyshire bread in the 16th century was rye-based, mixed with wheat and oats, sometimes barley, and even pea and bean flour to bulk out the meagre takings. White wheaten bread, known as manchet, was the stuff of the rich alone.

The Peak in Fitzherbert's time was very scarcely populated - just a few hill farmers and lead miners living in scattered hamlets. As a vivid illustration of this, in 1558 when a levy of 1,500 foot soldiers was demanded from the area the local argument was that the condition of the county would not allow it to raise more than 100.

On Holy Cross Day, Passion Flowers are supposed to bloom. Hidden somewhere in the patterns of these mystical flowers are symbols representing the Cross, the nails, the crown of thorns, the wounds of Christ, the apostles and Heaven itself. However, tracking down these blooms in the area might prove trickier than the average botanical jaunt...

16th - WEARING THE TROUSERS - WINSTER AND NEW MILLS

Cross-dressing, if not exactly mainstream these days, is certainly not something to hold the front page for. This was most definitely not the case in the 19th century, and it is the single-minded conviction and bravery of the following case that makes it worth re-committing to posterity, rather than the novelty value and prurience that immortalised it in the first place.

John Smith, part of a large Derbyshire family, was born in a cave - that's right, a cave - near Sutton in 1788. He was doing fine until he became involved in a Glossop pub brawl. During the ensuing ripping of clothes it became apparent to his assailant that John was a woman. Smith was able to continue in male guise, however, for records show that he later took £5 to marry a pregnant girl in order to save her reputation and, we must assume, shore up his own defences at the same time. The ceremony took place in Winster; but this was certainly not the last chapter in his family life. Several mistresses later John moved in with a new common-law wife and her 11 children at New Mills.

After examining John on his deathbed on this day in 1848, (he was dying of dysentery), a doctor commented on the patient's feminine features. He can't have looked that closely, though, for he failed to discover the full extent of the man's womanliness. The beans were spilled posthumously, although his faithful partner managed to get him buried before the full story emerged. Investigation revealed that John Smith had been born Sophia Locke, who had been dressed in boys' clothes since childhood. It was said that she had never grown out of the 'habit'. Today it sounds like a stroke of luck for a woman whose sexuality was not destined to follow the straight and narrow.

20th - RIGHT TO ROME - ALFRETON

According to the records of antiquary John Reynolds of Plaistow, Crich, a Roman hoard was discovered on this day in 1748, *'in a boggy piece of ground, near a watering place in ye lower close of a Farm, called New Grounds, near Green-hill lane, in ye Parish of Alfreton.'* It was discovered by Dan Elliot and a fellow farm labourer, whilst digging a drain. The men took the pot of around 1,500 silver coins to their master, Samuel Roe, who cleaned and sold it and divided the spoils three ways, in great secrecy so as not to fall foul of Treasure Trove laws.

However, the Lord of the Manor Rowland Morewood got to hear about the hoard and demanded the treasure for himself, as did the Countess Dowager of Oxford, who was Lady Paramount of the Hundred of Scarsdale in which the pot had been unearthed. Her steward offered to buy the silver back from those who had bought it (most of it having been sold in Nottingham) for 10 shillings per ounce. When the story went abroad, others flocked to the site, and it is estimated that another 500 coins were unearthed. The coins dated from the 2nd and 3rd centuries AD. Meanwhile, the threesome who took the original money appear to have evaded the law.

24th - POOR CHAMPION - EYAM

Benevolent spinster 'Miss Mompesson' died on this day in 1798. She was the last of the Mompessons by name, a family who achieved fame in tragic circumstances during the Eyam plague (August 25th).

Miss Mompesson was his great grand-daughter. Her friend Anna Seward (a forgotten poetess, very popular in her day and known as The Swan of Lichfield) suggests in an obituary that the spirit of the famous Rector was far from dead in his descendant: *'The poor around have lost a generous benefactress, attentive to all their wants, and watchfully interested in their welfare. Death never chilled a warmer heart, or translated a spirit of more spotless integrity.'*

27th - REMAINDERS OF MORTALITY - BOLSOVER

The grandly named Huntingdon Smithson of Bolsover died on this day in 1735. Famed as an architect, his epitaph in the local church records a slightly confused mixture of affection, guilt and a lack of essential commas:

Reader beneath this plaine stone buried ly
Smithsons remainders of mortality
Whose skill in architecture did deserve
A fairer tombe his memry to preserve
But since his nobler gifts of piety
To God to men justice and charity
Are gone to Heaven a building to prepare
Not made with hands his friends contented are
He here shall rest in hope till the world shall burne
And intermingle ashes with his urne

29th - St Michael's Day - WE FEW, WE CURFEW

This is more commonly known as Michaelmas. If it freezes before this date, it will continue to freeze after May 1st the following year, weatherlore would have you believe. It also tells us *'A dark Michaelmas, a light Christmas'*.

Known these days as little more than the name of one of the terms at posh schools, Michaelmas used to be the commonest day for the winter night curfew to begin - the first hint that winter was on the way. Curfew took the form of a tolling of the church bell, usually one strike for each of the days of the month that had passed in the current year and generally rung at 9pm.

The word itself may derive from the French *couvre feu*, meaning 'cover fire'. Curfew was, indeed, the time when household fires were supposed to be doused. The bell was tolled every night, apart from Sunday, until Shrove Tuesday. This is a generalisation - at Eyam, for example, curfew time was between October 29th and March 25th (see October 29th).

On the food front, chef recommends the goose - *'if you eat goose on Michaelmas Day you will never want money all the year round'*. Folklore says that this culinary trend was set by Queen Elizabeth who celebrated the defeat of the Spanish Armada in 1588 by tucking into a goose. The fact is goose had been traded and devoured at this time of year (between Michaelmas and Martinmas, November 11th) for centuries before. The most famous seasonal survival is the Nottingham Goose Fair on the first Thursday in October.

30th - SCOTS GO THROUGH BLACK HOLE - CHAPEL-EN-LE-FRITH

Not quite as famous as the Black Hole of Calcutta, the Black Hole of Derbyshire was the dubious nickname given to Chapel-en-le-Frith's church. It became the destination of some Scottish prisoners in 1648, the Scots having backed the wrong side in the English Civil War under the leadership of the Duke of Hamilton. Following their defeat at Preston in August, 1,500 prisoners were marched to Chapel and locked in the Black Hole for 16 days. On September 30th they were released. Forty four had died inside, and many more perished on the ensuing march to Chester. The church has since been restored, thus denying visitors the full Black Hole experience.

WIRKSWORTH

OCTOBER

1st - A STRANGE WAY TO DIE - DARLEY DALE

The Darley Dale registers note the following death:

'1612, Oct 1 - William Carlell, a strange beggar.'

In the same records we read the following terse obits:

'Ould Catharaine was buryed';

'James, son of Edmund Tatersall, a straunger';

'a maide from Sniterton Hall';

'A son of one Abill, a stranger and by trade a tinker'; and

'Anne, daughter of Samuel Giles, a stranger yt came out of Staffordshire'.

It makes for sad reading when posterity is not even left a full name to toy with. The terms 'Strange' and 'Stranger' were used for people who had not been born in the area, whilst beggars and travellers were usually labelled Vagrant or Peregrinus.

It is noticeable that in times of pestilence - the 1586-7 plague in Chesterfield, for example - such Vagrants are absent from the records. In other words, no-one was daft enough to enter plague areas from the outside.

2nd - A PLAGUE UPON YOUR 175 HOUSES - CHESTERFIELD

On the graves of Margaret Cade and her son John in Chesterfield is the note *'here began the great plague of Chesterfield'*. It was October 2nd 1586, and the plague ravaged the town for 14 months. It is reckoned that 175 of the 300 families living in Chesterfield at the time bore the brunt of the 347 deaths.

4th - BRAZEN THE STANDARD - WIRKSWORTH

Derbyshire lead miners were required by law to use a statutory measure for selling their washed and graded ore. The standard was set by a Miner's Dish or Measure, known more formally as the Lead Miner's Standard Dish.

The first of these standards was established with the Brazen Dish for the Wapentake of Wirksworth during the reign of Henry VIII, on this day in 1513. According to its Brazen inscription: *'this dishe to remayne in the Moote Hall at Wyrkysworth hanging by a chene so as the merchants or mynours may have resorte to the same at all tymes to make the trew measure after the same.'*

It contains about 14 pints, and remained the standard measure throughout the history of Derbyshire lead mining. (See Barmote Court, October 10th). And in case you are interested, nine dishes make a load, and four loads make a ton.

4th - St Francis' Day - HARD TO SWALLOW

On St Francis' Day swallows are supposed to fly to the bottom of ponds and hibernate through the winter. In the days before the idea of migration was understood, this seemed a reasonable explanation for their sudden disappearance. The fact that swallows skim the surface of ponds for insects may have been the starting point for this particular piece of folklore.

Traditionally a harbinger of good luck, a swallow brings instant misfortune if shot. It was once believed that the birds contained two magical stones, one black and one red. The black one bestows prosperity - but presumably not enough to offset the bad luck caused by shooting the bird to get the stone. The red stone cures insanity - and you would have to be mad to believe this stuff in the first place.

5th - St Faith's Eve - FAITH FULL OF CAKE

St Faith's Eve presents an opportunity for catching a glimpse of future loves.

Three women must watch over the baking of a Faith Cake (recipe optional), each of them turning it twice during the baking. Once cooked, the cake should be divided into three, and each third into nine. Each bit then has to be squished through the wedding ring of a woman married for at least seven years. The whole horrible mess must then be eaten, and you're allowed to talk with your mouth full as you cough and splutter through this verse:

> *Oh good St Faith be kind tonight*
> *And bring to me my heart's delight;*
> *Let me my future husband view*
> *And be my vision chaste and true.*

All you have to do then is hang the ring by your bed and sleep off the indigestion, dreaming as you do so of your future partner.

9th - CURE FOR CURATES - BREADSALL

George Holme, Vicar of Breadsall in the mid-17th century, was hauled before church authorities on this day in 1647. *'Carelessness and non-residence'* were just the beginning of his crimes, according to irate accusers, whose main complaint seems to be that the Vicar leaned towards the Royalists and High Church ways rather than the strict puritanism of the day.

Holme, they said, *'was very superstitious, used to bow towards the altar, did seldom preach... he hired curates that were drunkards, whoremasters or worse... and having once an honest curate, he turned him off... saying he would have no puritan under him and that he suffered the parsonage to go to great ruin and decay... One (curate) was a drunkard, another ran away being charged with a bastard and a third was indicted at Derby (but not committed) for buggery.'*

10th - RAKING UP THE DIRT - WIRKSWORTH

Lead mining has an ancient history in Derbyshire, and the miners, following centuries of oral law and tradition, were well organised from an early date. In 1255 their laws were, for the first time, set down in writing and approved by the King. The celebrated Court Barmote for the Lead Mines in Wirksworth dates from this time - its rules set it above the general laws of the land, with its own courts, officials and arcane customs.

The Barmote proceedings on this date in 1665 serve to illustrate the event. Solemn oaths were sworn by 24 signatories backing 59 rules for the guidance of miners, each commencing with the invocation *'We say that...'* After this all manner of mining-related issues were discussed, culminating in massed pipe smoking and a good supper.

At the court you could put forward complaints or discussions of any sort. Many of the customs were captured in Edward Manlove's 1653 catchily-titled book *Rhymed Chronicle of the Liberties and Customs of the Lead-mines within the Wapentake of Wirksworth.* Manlove was an ex-Steward of the Barmote Court. His purpose was to enable miners to learn the various rules and customs, in the belief that setting something to verse makes it easier to memorise. Not all of it is cheery stuff, mind:

> *For stealing ore twice from the minery*
> *The thief that's taken fined twice shall be;*
> *But the third time that he commits such theft*
> *Shall have a knife stuck thro' his hand to th' haft*
> *Into the stow, and there till death shall stand*
> *Or loose himself by cutting loose his hand.*
> *And shall foreswear the franchise of the mine*
> *And always lose his freedom from that time.*

The landscape at the time must have was very scarred, as you were allowed to dig wherever you found a lead 'rake' in the Wapentake of Wirksworth. With one or two exceptions, of course:

> *They may make crosses, holes, and set their stowes,*
> *Sink shafts, build lodges, cottages or coes.*
> *But churches, houses, gardens, all are free*
> *From this strange custom of the minery.*

In the 17th century Daniel Defoe wrote of his travels in the region, adding a note of grudging admiration to his customary derogatory tone. He mentions the trade of *'the Lead Workes, and of the subterranean Wretches... who work in the mines... they are a rude boorish kind of People, but they are bold, daring, and even desperate kind of Fellows in their Search into the Bowels of the Earth, for no People in the World outdo them.'*

Defoe also mentions the Barmote Court and its dealings with disputes and quarrels, which *'...in a word, keep the Peace among the miners... Which, by the way, may be called the greatest of all the Wonders of the Peak, for they are of a strange, turbulant, quarrellsome Temper, and hard to be reconciled to one another after their subterraneous affairs.'* Of Wirksworth in general the author was generous, describing *'the Provisions extraordinary good, not forgetting the Ale'*, a comment which put the local beer on the map for future wayfarers.

The Barmote Court still meets, and members still have a crafty smoke on their personalised, inscribed clay pipes. It is usually held in April these days, and you are probably not invited.

PLAQUE FROM THE BARMOTE COURT

11th - DEAD PARSON ON TORR - MONYASH

The Rev. Robert Lomas, Parson of Monyash, met a grim fate on October 11th 1776. His tale was later given a melodramatic setting in *The Legend of the Parson's Torr, Lathkill Dale*, penned in 1863 by the Rev W.R. Bell. A stormy night sets the scene, and we discover Parson Lomas sitting in his *'old oak armchair'*, fearful of the storm. He retires to bed, but cannot sleep. When he does eventually nod off, he dreams of falling into an abyss. The next day he rides to the church at Bakewell, the storm having passed. However, on the way home it begins to rain, and a misty drizzle covers the moors...

> *Ah! Thick was the mist on the moor that night,*
> *Poor wight, he had lost his way!*
> *The north-east wind blowing strong on his right,*
> *To the left had made him stray...*
>
> *Still onward and leeward, at last he came*
> *To the edge of Harlow Dale;*
> *From his cave the Lathkill a warning roared,*
> *But louder then howled the gale.*

On the brink of Fox Torr the doomed man stood,
And tugged the bridle in vain;
His horse would not move - then quick started back,
And, snap, went each bridle-rein!

Then headlong fell he o'er the lofty cliff,
He shrieked, and sank in the gloom;
Down - down to the bottom he swiftly sped,
And death was his dreadful doom.

His servant Betty then spots his mournful ghost as she is milking, and realises that he must have come to grief. A search party gathers on the 12th:

At last the searchers went into the Dale,
And there at the foot of Fox Torr -
They found the parson, all cold and dead,
'Mong the rocks all stained with gore.

Fox Torr was renamed Parson's Torr on the strength of it. A macabre memento of the incident - a handful of grass found clutched in the desperate man's hand - was preserved into the middle of the 19th century, allegedly.

It would have been neither here nor there to the poor Parson to know from which direction the aforementioned gale was blowing. However, the rest of us are enthralled to hear weatherlore's assurances that a west wind on the 12th presages a spell of fine weather ahead.

14th - St Calistus' Day - WINTER WONDERLAND

According to the old runestick almanacs (see April 14th), St Calistus' Day is the beginning of Winter, which lasts through until April 13th. It was thus the first day on the 'Winterside' of the sticks, and its symbol was a fir tree. Elsewhere in folklore winter begins later in the month, on St Simon and St Jude's Day (28th), heralding the onset of wet and windy weather. We residents of Buxton remain unalarmed by the prospect of yet more inclement weather.

14th - EYRES AND GRACES - HOPE

The coat of arms of the land-owning Eyre family of Hope Valley depicts a single leg above a shield. Sounds like a cue for a daft legend...

It was October 14th 1066, and the Battle of Hastings was still very much undecided. At a turning point in the melee, William the would-be Conqueror was knocked from his horse and lay winded on the ground, his helmet restricting his breathing and his life in genuine danger. He was saved by the quick-thinking of a fellow Norman called Truelove, who pulled off the helmet.

William asked the name of his saviour, and on receiving the answer 'Truelove' he was blessed, for the first and last time in his life, with the ability to speak English (and in 19th century tones at that), declaring: *'From now on, Truelove shall be called Eyre, for you have given me the 'Air' to breathe!'*

Towards the end of the battle William checked on the progress of his champion Eyre, only to discover that the man had one less leg than he had arrived with. The almost-Conqueror declared that he would award Eyre for his bravery and courage with a large chunk of the English midlands. *'Then I shall call it Hope'*, Eyre replied, *'For your words have given me the hope to live!'* The family has been ensconced in the Hope Valley ever since.

16th - HOW TO FORGE PERPETUAL MOTION - CHELMORTON

The notion of Perpetual Motion has been pursued by inspired mathematicians down the centuries; and Derbyshire has not been without its contenders.

Owd Alick was a Chelmorton blacksmith and landlord appropriately of the Blacksmith's Arms. Having done his sums, Alick, aka Alexander Ollerenshaw, spent many years trying to perfect a machine which would prove his theories. When challenged as to his sanity, he would quote Sir Isaac Newton who, in Alick's words, declared that *'perpetual motion would be found out, and the discovery would be made by an idiot'*. Owd Alick died on this day in 1841, his prize having eluded him.

Mid-October - MAGNA CHARTER - ILKESTON

Founded over 750 years ago, Ilkeston Charter Fair is one of the oldest street fairs in Europe. Like other events of its kind it has lost its former identity as a market (if you ignore the burger and candyfloss vendors), but continues to thrive as a four-day funfair. Originally held on the Festival of the Assumption (August 15th), in 1888 it was combined with the town's Hiring Fair and Wakes Week in October. Since 1931 the Fair has been opened by the Mayor of Erewash, who rings a hand bell and addresses the eager crowd.

18th - St Luke's Day

St Luke's Day is often at the centre of a spell of particularly fine weather known as St Luke's Little Summer. St Luke's was also known as Dog Whipping Day, when all the stray dogs in the streets had to be whipped out of town. They were probably used to it, as many towns and villages had permanent dog-whippers to belabour the curs every week of the year (see Feb. 5th).

21st - NON-SILENT KNIGHT

The Statham family of Tideswell and Wigwall were a force to be reckoned with in the 18th century. John Statham was knighted in 1714, and was famous for his vigorous and quarrelsome nature. On this day in 1730 he wrote back to someone who had, clearly, given him some of his own medicine: *'I am amazed at the unbecoming language... I can't guess what I said to provoke you, can't apprehend it other than some accidental overheat of blood; it amazes me that a person of your understanding and a perfect master of words should use language only fit for miners and footmen in a common Alehouse amongst the dregs of mankind.'*

In the same year he put his lands up for let, calling them *'the finest part of England for Health, Hunting, Shooting, & other Diversions. The only Epidemical Distemper that ills the Inhabitants there is Age.'* Living his life in a whirl of arrogance and vitriol, it is hardly surprising that John Statham managed to fall out with his family, as evinced by his own suggested epitaph:

My Epitaph.
Under this stone there lies a knight,
With cares and sorrows kill'd outright.
His thread was not quite run,
His died by a graceless son.
Parents beware! And take his word,
That greffe will kill without a word.

The last line is a clever irony, coming from a man renowned for his murderous verbal ability. However, self-pity had kicked in by now, and in 1757 Statham made a statement beginning *'Whilst the Devil and evil spirits have power in the world, so long will Envy, Malice, Lies & Distraction continue... No person in this County has suffered more by vile calumnies than Sir John Statham, who for many years has been the mark at which the Faction have shot their envenomed Arrows, & bent their whole Efforts...'*

The gist of the rapidly purpling prose is that Sir John vows to redress any wrong that can be proved against him - or he promises to prosecute for slander.

23rd - KING PAYS DEERLY - DALE ABBEY

Dale Abbey in Deep Dale was dissolved this day in 1539. Nothing but a ruined window arch can be seen now, plus a font which was rescued by Dale church and a stained glass window removed to Morley church. Legend says that the original Hermitage was founded by a Derby baker who had visions of the Blessed Virgin, telling him to seek out Deep Dale. When he located the marshy spot in AD1130 he hollowed out a cave from the sandstone, and devoted his life to God. He evaded the predictable temptations of Satan (appearing as a woman, etc.), aided by the local landowner Ralph Fitz-Geremund.

The land later fell to holy woman Gomme of the Dale, and her tonsured son

Richard. By now there was a Chapel at Deep Dale, and the Abbey was built there in 1204. A certain Prior Robert had been told by King John that the Abbey could claim as much land as two plough-pulling wild deer could encircle between sunrise and sunset. They did, of course, manage to plough like no deer before or since, (as depicted in the above-mentioned stained glass window).

The link with Robert, who is actually St Robert of Knaresborough, is doubtful; but he was one of the most famous and crowd-pulling saints in the early 13th century, and any Abbey in need of pilgrims would have welcomed - if not positively invented - such legends.

25th - ANOTHER FINE MESSE - WILLIAM CAVENDISH

William Cavendish was a leading local Derbyshire nobleman at the time of the Dissolution in the late 1530s, from which he profited shamelessly. Soon enough, however, he was facing the prospect of finding out how God felt about all this tampering with religion and property. Death takes no prisoners, but in a vain attempt to woo the dying Cavendish back to health in 1557, a special menu was prepared, consisting of Necks of Mutton, Pigeons, Oysters, Whiting, Capons, Calf's-foot jelly, and repeated doses of Wormwood Wine.

Household bills a few days later mention 20 pennies *'for seyinge Messe - to a preste and to the Clarke'*, so the food had clearly not done the trick. Cavendish died on the 25th; but as far as we know he didn't panic as much as Henry VIII, whose last words were: *'All is lost! Monks, monks, monks...'*

28th - FATHER DAN KEEPS THE FLAGON FLYING - DALE ABBEY

Sticking with the monastic theme... When Father Dan John Stanley the Abbot of Dale Abbey retired, he was having nothing to do with abstinence and austerity. He claimed a big fat pension from the profits of the Abbey-held land. According to the agreement drawn up on this day in 1491, DJS was allowed to keep his old chambers at the Abbey, with *'annual doles of wood, coal, candles, plus sufficient loaves of the best paste made in our monastery, and victuals wholesome for him and sufficient for his sustenance from our kitchen, namely, dishes of meat and fish and other victuals according as the day shall require; and, weekly, eight flagons of the best beer for his drinking to be provided at our expense and determined for him wherever such beer can be obtained and provided in the surrounding towns and places near our Abbey.'*

Father Dan was also allotted two servants, pasture for two horses, plus essential household items, all of which reverted to the Abbey upon his death.

29th - WATCH & WARD - EYAM

Eyam's Watch and Ward used to commence on this night, in conjunction with the village's curfew bell. Watch and Ward was a rota of night-sentries, and all male householders had to take it in turns *'guarding'* the Lydgate, which is the main road into the village. (For more on curfew, see September 29th).

30th - GOING TO THE GIG - NEWHAVEN

Newhaven used to hold its Gig Fair on this day, a livestock and general produce market, with the usual rich mix of sideshows and quacks. Local farm-workers and servants were given a holiday, possibly to discourage the unofficial holiday of Mischief Night on Hallowe'en. The word 'gig' means fun and merriment.

31st - Hallowe'en - WHICH IS WITCH?

Having faded in England due to Guy Fawkes Night in the 17th century, Hallowe'en, via re-export from America, is now a cult again. Also known as All Hallows or All Saints Eve, Hallowe'en was the eve of the Celtic New Year, the feast of Samhain. Superstitions associated with the season made a seamless transition from pagan to Christian. Being New Year, Samhain offers us glimpses into the future, should we care to peek. In Derbyshire girls used to put sprigs of rosemary under their pillows to dream of future husbands.

Rowan wood is the principle protection at the dangerous All Hallows season, seeing off both witches and fairies. The local name for this tree, wiggan, comes from the Old English *wice,* or *wican* - rowan. It survives in the Derbyshire place names Wiggon Shea (Shottle) and Wiggin Dale (Bakewell). The wood acts as a powerful charm against witchcraft, the Evil Eye, travelling salesmen, etc. It was used in the manufacture of farm implements, including the butter churn staff - to prevent butter being spoilt by witchery.

Not all tonight's skulduggery is engineered by witchery and fairies; Hallowe'en used to be observed as Mischief Night in much of the region - an excuse for stealing gates, knocking on doors and running away ('knick-knocking'), dolloping drawing-pin laden dung onto door handles, and several unsavoury, and probably equally alliterative, things besides.

The ancient custom of leaving food offerings for family spirits returning from the grave survived in the Matlock region until the early 20th century. These days, with fancy-dress extravaganzas and trick-or-treaters stalking every street and bar in the land, irate ancestors are the least of your worries.

BRADFORD DALE

NOVEMBER

1st - All Saints Day - ALL SAINTS, HALF A CHURCH

November 1st is the feast of All Saints or All Hallows - Hallow Day as opposed to Hallow E'en. The feast is a commemoration not just of all the saints that ever existed, but of every last redeemed soul believed to be in Heaven.

All Saints was always a popular church dedication, and there are more edifices of that name in England than any other (following the anti-Catholic loss of many churches dedicated to St Mary). Derbyshire has its fair share, with churches of All Saints at Ashover, Aston-on-Trent, Bakewell, Bradbourne, Breadsall, Chesterfield, Dalbury, Dale Abbey, Heath and Sudbury, plus Mickleover and Mackworth in the Derby suburbs, and several others, including the cathedral in Derby itself. The latter has enjoyed cathedral status since 1927, in a town which only received official city status in 1977.

Chesterfield was clearly torn between which of the two commonest dedications to choose, opting for the dual matron/patronage of Our Lady and All Saints. All the churches in the above list contain gems worth tracking down, even the mid-Victorian example at Heath which has Anglo-Saxon carvings on display.

Special mention should be made of the edifice at Dale Abbey - a tiny building half church and half farmhouse (a former pub) containing a rare mediaeval wall painting.

2nd - All Souls Day - BLESS MY SOUL

The customs of All Souls Day (commemorating the souls of everyone alive, dead and yet to come) are steeped in the Samhain traditions of the Hallowe'en season.

The day was known in Derbyshire and South Yorkshire as Cakin' Neet. Alms-collectors would don crude Hallowe'en-style masks and beg from door to door for *'cake, cake, copper, copper, cake, cake.'* The usual reward for this was a slice of parkin and some loose change. It was also customary to hold services in the churchyards, and to leave cake offerings for the dead.

The ancient notion of 'sin-eating' lies behind this otherwise bizarre link between cakes and the dead. By eating a cake which has been passed over the grave of a dead person, the diner ingests some of that person's sins, thereby lessening their stint in the hot limbo flames of Purgatory.

The Cakin' Neet masks-and-alms rituals managed to hang on in the South Yorkshire borderlands of Dungworth and Stannington. Keep your ear to the ground and an eye on the press, and you may still be able to encounter the Cakers in their bizarre fancy dress.

All Souls was the day for kindling the Tindles at Findern, which isn't very easy to say. This was, originally, linked to the notion of Purgatory once again. Children would light fires in the furze on Findern common, and these were said to act as a light, guiding souls from Purgatory at this ghostly and restless time of year. The whole notion probably pre-dates Christianity by a religion or two. 'Tindle' itself means a fire, from the dialect word tind, which has the same Anglo-Saxon origin as the 'tinder' in 'tinder-box', and means 'to kindle'.

In Lancashire the name for the custom was teanlay or teanla, and this obscure but widespread word is found in various forms throughout many UK regions, and also in old Scandinavian, Germanic and French languages. Hereby endeth the etymology lesson. Meanwhile, the Enclosure Acts put an end to Tindles, which relied on the old Common land, and it sputtered out in the second half of the 19th century.

3rd - SPINNING A YARN - THE MINSTREL OF THE PEAK

William Newton, The Minstrel of the Peak, died on this day in 1830, aged 80. He is buried in Tideswell churchyard. A locally significant cog in the Industrial Revolution, heavily involved in the Derbyshire cotton industry, Newton was befriended by well-to-do poetess Anna 'Swan of Lichfield' Seward. It was Seward who applied the 'Minstrel' tag.

True to the conventions of the time, this type of patronage was genuinely patronising. Sewards's first description of William Newton is typical of the manner in which the upper middle classes viewed the rest of us. She says he is *'not ill-looking, but has nothing in his appearance beyond the decent and clean... he conversed, though in the accent of his own county... the ease and elegance of his epistolary style are most extraordinary, his birth and uneducated youth considered... To have found, in the compositions of a laborious villager, some bright sparks of genius amid the dross of prosaic vulgarity had been pleasing, though perhaps not wonderful; but the elegance and harmony of Newton's writings, both in prose and verse, are miraculous when it is remembered that... he had only associated with the unlettered vulgar.'*

It has since been argued that Seward was only swanning around with the working class poet to bolster her posthumous reputation as a liberal-minded patroness of the under-privileged. As advisor and stylist she had nothing positive or enhancing to offer Newton.

The poetry remained a hobby for the Minstrel of the Peak. In mid-life his day job involved a three mile walk over the moor from Tideswell to Monsal Dale to reach the cotton mill where he worked as a machinery carpenter for £50 a year. A poem of around 1785 describes the journey:

> *Yet here, on Tideswell's wintry moor*
> *While drifted snow my steps ensnare,*
> *And through the nights the tempests roar,*
> *And fiercely whirl my frozen hair;*
>
> *As straggling, towards my home I wend,*
> *Sweet fancy cheers the dreary way,*
> *On my chill'd heart her fires descend,*
> *Bright as the star that leads the day...*
>
> *Me Julia's friendship cheers each morn;*
> *Truth whispers it shall never last;*
> *Then let me present evils scorn,*
> *And bravely triumph o'er the past.*

When the mill burnt down (on November 15th 1785), Newton lost his tools, and nearly his life. Millowner Richard Arkwright sacked him, unfairly blaming him for the blaze, and feeling petulant due to the fact that the mill was uninsured.

Anne Seward raised money to save her Minstrel from ignominy. Afterwards he became a cotton manufacturer-cum-manager at Cressbrook - a mill which he helped construct - and enjoyed a charitable reputation, notably towards his child employees (in contrast to the nightmare reports of their treatment at nearby Litton Mill).

Newton's admirers called him the Derbyshire Wordsworth, and his best work captures the essence and moods of the hills and moors. Like Seward, however, he is little regarded now. He should be properly remembered, all poetical considerations apart, as the man who helped bring about the abolition of gibbeting in the county (April 1st), and for documenting the Derbyshire countryside and the tribulations of the poor factory workers in their struggle for dignity and tolerable lives.

4th - PUB REVOLUTION - WHITTINGTON

Revolution House at Whittington (now a suburb of Chesterfield) was an unprepossessing building that just happened to be the spot where several history-makers got together in 1688. William Cavendish, The Earl of Devonshire, met the Earl of Danby and other gentlemen here to discuss what to do about James II and his pro-Catholic, anti-Parliament policies.

The result was the Glorious Revolution and the Bill of Rights. This curtailed the unlimited powers of royalty, tied the Stuarts to a staunch Protestant agenda, and, after the failure of 'Orange' William III and Mary Stuart to produce a dynasty, ushered in the accession of the not-very-British Hanoverians.

The conspirators used a meeting of the Whittington Moor hunt as a front for their clandestine conference, congregating at an inn called the Cock and Pynot. Only after the event did posterity seek out this epoch-making inn. It was renovated and extended in 1769, when it became known as Revolution House, the centenary shindig on November 4th 1788 finally putting the place on the national map.

The French Revolution, however, brought violent disrepute to the R-word in aristocratic circles, and the place fell into relative obscurity again. A low-key celebration was held in 1888 and a bronze commemorative tablet was installed, with the words: *'A.D. 1688. In a room which formerly existed at the end of this cottage (what is left of the old Cock and Pynot) the Earl of Danby, The Earl of Devonshire and John D'Arcy (eldest son of the Earl of Holderness) met some time in 1688 to concert measures which resulted in the Revolution of that year.'*

Revolution House still stands, and is now a fascinating museum.

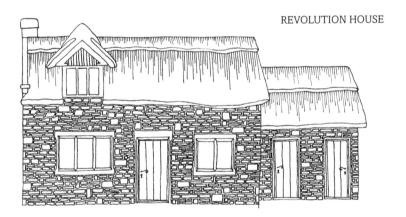

REVOLUTION HOUSE

4th - JOLLY JAPES - CASTLETON AND TIDESWELL

Bonfire Night Eve was observed as Mischief Night in some Peak District villages, including Castleton. High jinks were the order of the evening, and youths would carry their hormones and adrenaline from street to street playing annoying put hopefully harmless pranks on locals by removing, befouling and hitting various objects and items of property. Similar things, in certain places, occurred at Hallowe'en and Christmas Eve.

Bonfire Night Eve was far more practical and organised in several north-east Derbyshire and South Yorkshire villages. Here, children would engage in a bout of

Jolly Minering. A local variant on Penny for the Guy traditions, the aim was to raise money for sweets and fireworks. Their alms-song started like this:

We're three Jolly Miners, and we're not worth a pin,
So give us a piece of coal and we'll make the kettle sing.

The song itself comes from an earlier time when the aim of the activity was to gather coal, either for the 'bonfire hole', or simply to light a fire to cook and 'make the kettle sing'. A Tideswell variant on the theme runs:

Coal, coal, a bonfire hole,
A stock and a stake for King George's sake
If you please will you give me a penny
For my bonfire hole.

5th - 'GUY FAWKES' RINGS A BELL - BONFIRE NIGHT

Bell-ringers usually held their annual feast on November 5th, and church records reveal that it was one of the year's most expensive outlays.

At St Werburgh's in Derby, for example, apart from essential clock repairs, the £1 9s 6d for Guy Fawkes bell-ringing is the priciest thing in the institution's 17th century records. For comparison, an Oak Apple Day peal (29th May) in 1666, and the ringing which celebrated the Treaty of Breda in 1667 each cost a mere three shillings and sixpence. Even ringing-in the new King in 1685 was only five shillings.

The same King's birthday on April 1st that year warranted a meagre 6d *'for the ringers' ale'*. Perhaps these paltry sums are a reflection on the unpopular James II, who was destined to be ousted from office three years later (November 4th).

Tonight is, of course, famous for commemorating the anniversary of the capture of Guy Fawkes and his fellow Gunpowder Plotters. Traditional Bonfire Night foodstuffs have always been the order of the night. In much of Derbyshire, Thar Cake (aka Tharf or Thor Cake) was the traditional sweet treat on November 5th - and, indeed, during the whole Samhain season (see October 31st). The cakes are a variation on parkin, with oatmeal, fruit peel, lots of treacle, and ginger or caraway. The cutting and handing out of the sticky stuff in individual households was known as Thar Cake Joining. Gingerbread, similar but different, is another Sahmain/Bonfire Night delicacy. The famous Gingerbread Shop in Ashbourne is the place to go for the genuine article.

It is tempting to link Thar cakes to the God Thor, once worshipped in this former portion of the Danelaw. The notion is backed up by the presence of the impressive Thor's Cave in the Manifold Valley. It is even claimed that November 5th is the ever-popular thunder god's feast day. However, Thar probably derives from the Old English *theorf*, meaning unleavened.

Bonfires used to blaze in the county's many market squares today. The charred market cross at Chapel-en-le-Frith is evidence of the practice; and this town was one of the last to observe the in-the-streets version of the custom. At Dove Holes an annual bonfire used to be lit in the centre of the impressive (if stoneless) henge monument known as The Bull Ring, until archaeologists suggested in the 1980s that this might not be such a good idea.

Large, organised bonfires still survive, usually on the nearest weekend; although in recent years insurance problems have threatened even these vestiges. The U.S.-led litigious society of the 21st century is sounding the death knell for many ancient customs: unless someone comes up with a way of stemming the inexorable and depressing flow, bonfires, carnivals and other communal celebrations are doomed.

6th - WHIPPING UP CUSTOM - DERBY

Public whipping was a common street spectacle in the mid-19th century. A contributor to *The Derbyshire and Nottinghamshire Notes and Queries,* comments in passing, in the March 1894 edition: *'In the year 1825, I saw a man flogged at a cart tail in Walker Lane'.* The lane is in Derby, and it was noted at that time for its dubious characters.

In Derby and elsewhere, market day was the best time to observe the quaint old custom of unisex public flogging.

6th - FILLING FULWOOD FULL OF LEAD - BRADFORD DALE

Fulwood's Cave, also known as Cromwell's Cave, is near Middleton in Bradford Dale. It is the spot where Royalist Christopher Fulwood was fatally wounded by his Parliamentarian adversaries during the English Civil War.

Fulwood had caused great concern to the Roundheads after managing to muster 1,100 men to fight for Charles I. Most of them were from the mining community, Fulwood owning one of the richest veins of lead in the county. When the tide turned against the King, the Parliamentary Governor for Derbyshire John Gell sent men to arrest Fulwood. He fled to the cave, but was shot, and he died on the way to imprisonment on this day in 1643.

7th - ANY JUST IMPEDIMENT...? - WINSTER

In Winster Church on this day in 1308, a certain consanguinity was called into question. It was argued that Richard, son of Stafford de Eyam, and his wife Isabella, should not legally have been married, on account of being too closely related. Several witnesses came forward to prove as convincingly as they could that the couple, if not quite brother and sister, were still peas from the same pod.

Poor Richard and Isabella were, indeed, divorced on the strength of the case, although the evidence shows them to have been no more or less related than the parties of any other aristocratic union. Their respective grandparents were cousins, i.e. their great grandparents were brothers. Hardly the most desperate case of inbreeding in history's annals.

Early November - MANY HANDS MAKE LIGHT WORK - DERBY DIWALI

Derby's Hindu and Sikh community celebrates the five-day moveable feast of Diwali, the 'Row of Lights', in and around the city during early November. The festival celebrates the victory of good over evil, light over darkness, and knowledge over ignorance. Decorative lights straddle the streets, and householders place personal lamps in their windows; while traditional Diwali sweets and fireworks keep the children happy.

This ancient festival of light is said to mark the return from exile of King Rama, one of the many manifestations of the god Vishnu. Other deities honoured at Diwali include Vishnu's consort Laksmi, a four-armed Lotus Goddess who sports a very fetching elephant's trunk.

10th - HOT EYRE - HOPE

In the latter half of the 16th century disputes flared up between two powerful local clans, the Eyres and the Woodruffes. They were closely related, of course, as was ever the case with aristocracy. In the mid 1550s the absurdly wealthy Humphrey Stafford had died, leaving a vast estate to his four daughters. Their ensuing marriages set the scene for the rivalries to come, with a righteous indignation based on that thing which, of all the folk of Derbyshire, those families had the least to worry about - money.

The youngest daughter, Gertrude, had three husbands, the first being a Woodruffe. After his early retirement to the afterlife she remarried, taking certain annuities, formerly paid to the Woodruffes, with her. When, later still, she married an Eyre, those annuities came back to haunt her ex-kin.

In 1591 the ill feeling came to a head. Rowland Eyre and Edmund Woodruffe had been fighting pettily over grazing rights, the root of the dispute being that niggling annuity, which the Woodruffes now refused to pay to Gertrude and her Eyre partner Rowland. Eyre sent men onto the hills and moors to round up and capture Woodruffe cattle, and the opposition played tit for tat.

On November 10th the Woodruffe faction stocked up on Dutch courage in a Hope pub, and in the fight that followed an Eyre employee was killed. The matter went straight to the Star Chamber, and an out-of-court order was served on Edmund Woodruffe. The nature of the order shocked him into promising to give Rowland Eyre a lump sum representing the outstanding annuities.

Woodruffe's hand had been forced in the matter, and he went on record with a statement insisting that by this agreement he would be *'utterly undone and never able to stand upon his head'* afterwards. Head-stands or not, he was not exactly destined for destitution and the workhouse, unlike the majority of his employees.

11th - Martinmas - NO CAKES, NO SUMMER, NOVEMBER

The feast of St Martin, Martinmas - known locally as Martlemas - was a time for hiring fairs, at which farm labourers would seek new posts. It was also the time when autumn wheat seeding was usually completed in many places, including the south of Derbyshire. Here it was the farmer's custom to provide a cakes-and-ale feast for workers. The special cakes were made with seeds and whole grains, and called Hopper Cakes. (April 25th).

Beef was the day's traditional meat dish. However, it is a long time since anyone finished sowing in November, and as early as 1894 a correspondent to *The Nottinghamshire and Derbyshire Notes and Queries* wrote: *'I am afraid even to guess how many years it is since the boon was given.'* Since 1918 the 11th has been commemorated as Armistice Day, and all remnants of the old Martinmas celebrations have disappeared.

ST MARTIN

St Martin is associated with the thermal spring at Stoney Middleton, although its fame pre-dates Christianity. A ruined 18th century bath house stands over the water source, and it is thought to have been used in a similar capacity by the Romans.

Martinmas supposedly heralds a spell of fine weather known as St Martin's Summer. This is God's commemoration of the fact that Martin once gave his warm cloak to a freezing beggar. If the good weather fails to materialise, the consolation is that a cold St Martin's leads to a gentle winter. It is also said that whichever way the wind blows today, it will stick there for the rest of the year.

Rector Thomas Moseley of Darley Dale had every right to view the promise of St Martin's Summer cynically. In 1676 he wrote in the parish registers:

A great ffrost which Began at Martinmas, was continued till January 3, 1677. Derwent was accordingly ffrozen, and att ye dissolving of the ffrost was a great fflood, and incredible quantity of Ice were brought out of the water-bankes into tollerable inclosed grounds, and up to the Church-yard steps.

14th - UNFAIR GAME - ENCLOSURES

Once upon a time common land yielded common resources for everyone with wit, skill and patience enough to take advantage of them. Then came the Enclosures, shutting off the rich supplies of rabbits, grazing land and suchlike. The inevitable poaching which followed was, of course, vilified in both town and country. In 1751, the following indictment was published in Derby:

'Whereas the Game in this County, is Daily destroyed by common Poachers, and loose Idle People, in so notorious a manner, that even Gentlemen of the largest Estates cannot find Game enough to their own... We whose names are hereunto subscribed do jointly and severally agree to punish all offenders in general against the Laws now in Force for the better Preservation of all Game...'

The High Sheriff and the Duke of Devonshire head the list of self-serving toffs. The rank and file of the population might well have mused along these lines, taken from a slightly later Nottinghamshire folk song:

A buck or doe, believe it so, a pheasant or a hare
Were put on earth for everyone quite equal for to share...

15th - PUB DETAILS LEEKED

The unimpressed Sir Francis Leek, JP, signed and sealed a census of the licensed premises of Derbyshire on this day in 1577, representing *'...the number and names of all as keep any alehouses, inns and taverns within this county of Derby whereof many are very poor.'*

The county's tally was as follows: Derby had 61 alehouses, two taverns and seven inns. Elsewhere in the county there were 726 alehouses, five taverns and 18 inns.

As to the distinctions, alehouses specialised in beer, and taverns (or vyntners in Leek's records) sold wine. The most esteemed of the outlets were the inns, which provided food and accommodation in addition to the booze. The 'very poor' tag applied to the poverty of the landlords rather than the quality of the drink. In many modern pubs it is all too often the other way round.

19th - GENUINE REPRODUCTION - NORBURY

The following epitaph can be found at the Church in Norbury, from 1473:

> *The body that beried is under this stone*
> *Of Nichol Fitzherbert Lord and Patrone*
> *Of Norbury with Alis the daughter of Henry Bothe*
> *Eight sonnes and five daughters he had in sothe*
> *Two sonnes and two daughters by Isabel his wyfe*
> *So seventeen Children he had in his lyfe*
> *This Church he made of his own expence*
> *In the Joy of Heaven be his recompence*
> *And in moone of November the nineteenth dey*
> *He bequeathed his Soule to everlasting jey.*

(see July 24 for more on Fitzherbert)

25th - St Catherine's Day - PARISH'S STAR TURN

Amongst the long matter-of-fact lists of baptisms, weddings and burials in the Parish Registers of Morley and Smalley, the following breathless snippets appear:

'1618. Memorand. That this yeare Novemb the 25th and for three weekes after, the blazing starre appeared in the East and did retrogade. January the 11th the Whitehall was burned and Queen Anne died the spring followinge.'

After that it was back to business with those baptisms, weddings, etc. None of which would have affected the truth, or otherwise, of the following weatherlore:

> *As at Catherine foul or fair*
> *So will be next Februeer.*

Knowing that November 25th is St Catherine's Day, and knowing how to make February rhyme with fair, are equally vital in deciphering this rhyme.

25th - TAKE NOTE - *DERBYSHIRE NOTES & QUERIES*

On this date in 1871 the first *Derbyshire Notes and Queries* appeared in the Derbyshire Times. This marks the beginning of the ongoing tradition of noting down local customs, traditions and trivia via articles, questions and proposed answers. In 1892 the popular section escaped the confines of the newspaper and, joining forces with Nottinghamshire, became a fully fledged publication in its own right.

Rev. J. Charles Cox, the *Nottinghamshire and Derbyshire Notes and Queries* editor, comments in his introduction to that first volume in 1892: *'There are... some desirable correspondents whose dignity would scarcely permit them to write to a penny paper, who will be well content to have their communications enshrined within the pages of a decent magazine.'*

Snobbery, dignity and apathy conspired to doom the well-meaning endeavour, and *Notes and Queries* struggled constantly for money and contributors throughout its brief reign. It is, however, true to say that without that magazine, tracking down information for this present book would have been far more difficult.

30th - POACHED SQUIRREL - DUFFIELD

The concept of Free Warren is common to most counties. It is the time when, by unofficial law, commoners are able to take to the fields and woods and gather whatever they can for the family cooking pot.

November 30th was a popular day for observing the tradition; unless you happened to be a landowner or gamekeeper, of course. In many places the custom was known as Squirrel Hunting. This was the case at Duffield, Stanton-in-the-Peak and elsewhere. At Duffield youths armed with drums, horns and other means of making noise descended on Kedleston Park and captured as many squirrels as they could. The animals were then released in the streets of the town, and the rodents who got caught a second time were destined for pies.

More tellingly, the hunters would also take a cart along, gathering precious firewood; and you can rest assured that they did not limit their wildlife attentions to the squirrels.

BRADWELL

DECEMBER

1st - VERNON HAS THE GUTS TO BE BURIED IN LONDON - SUDBURY

John Harestaffe, author of the eccentric *Rhymed Chronicle*, died on this day in 1645. His *Chronicle* concerns the everyday shenanigans, dull and fascinating alike, of the Vernon family of Sudbury Hall. Harestaffe composed his opus between 1615 and 1635 whilst living in the household, which he first entered in 1591 as John Vernon's servant.

Harestaffe, a bachelor, proved a most devoted assistant, and in John Vernon's will of 1600 he was rewarded for his efforts with a farm at Rodsley. His *Rhyming Chronicle*, along with other family-related literature, has become known as Vernoniana.

The *Chronicle* is in pentameter rhyming couplets, dealing with John Vernon, his wife and children, the people who gained from his generous will, Harestaffe himself, and the legal trials and tribulations of John Vernon's widow Mary and her revolting tenants. The chronicler also touches upon two nationally famous men of the time - Sir Robert Cecil, and the Earl of Essex, who was executed in 1601.

A biographical essay on Harestaffe written for *The Derbyshire Archaeological Journal* in 1888 fails to muster much praise for the quality of the man's verses: *'The muse of John Harestaffe may not be very brilliant, though, compared with the literature of the age it need by no means be despised.'* His use of rhyme to record family details is a whimsical exercise rather than an attempt to conjure artful poetry from prosaic events. The Rodsley inheritance from John Vernon proved to be a controversial issue. John Harestaffe himself had written down his master's last will and testament, and it was argued afterwards that he had prejudiced the issue in order to receive the farm. The *Chronicle* touches briefly on the issue:

> *[The farm] to Harestaffe and his heires should be convey'd*
> *For ever. Which although it was gain-said*
> *At first, yet after was it soe assur'd*
> *To recompence his travayles longe endured.*

One of the most interesting sections concerns the handling of Vernon's corpse after his death in London:

> *Most friends advys'd his bodie to interre,*
> *At some nere place, as Paules or Westminster:*
> *His mournfull wyffe in noe wyse would consent*
> *Thereto: because it was her full intent,*
>
> *He should in such a place interred be,*
> *Where after death herself might also lye.*
> *She therefore caus'd his bodie be prepar'd*
> *And drest with odors sweete noe cost she spar'd*

His Bowells to Westham were first convey'd
And in the Parish Church were buried:
And then his Corpes with full solemnitie
To her great charge were brought to Sudbury...

There are no church records at West Ham (London) prior to 1653, and no other tradition or knowledge of Vernon's bowels being buried there. It does, however, seem highly unlikely that the matter-of-fact Harestaffe would invent something so morbid. (See June 24th and March 25th).

1st - PAPER AND OTHER MATERIAL - DERBY

On this day in 1719 Derbyshire's first printed newspaper, *The Derby Post-Man*, appeared. It was a weekly, and cost thruppence ha'penny. The paper contained no local news or local advertisements, but thrilled its readers with *'a Collection of the most material Occurences, Foreign and Domestick; Together with An Account of Trade.'*

3rd - St Cecilia's Eve - CECILIA, YOU'RE BREAKING MY HEART

Marry on December third
For all the grief you ever heard,

So says folklore. This seemingly arbitrary superstition was common to several counties besides Derbyshire. It is hard to pin down its origin; although today is St Cecilia's Eve according to the pre-Gregorian calendar, and third-century Cecilia was famous for taking a Christian vow of chastity after her marriage.

A bout of early snow may well firm your marital resolve, however, as an old rhyme tells us:

When December snows fall fast
Marry and true love will last.

5th - A LOT OF BRIDES - DERBY WIFE-SELLING

Marrying on December 5th doesn't carry any bad luck, as far as I know. It is, however, difficult to guess the state of mind of the former Mrs Bott on this day in 1772. In Derby's market place she was sold by her husband Thomas to a man from Langley Common. The knock-down price was 18d.

The tradition of wife-selling may seem to have little to recommend it; but a couple of things need bearing in mind. If a marriage was bringing misery to the parties involved, such a 'sale' was the only accepted way out. Divorce, prior to the establishment of a Divorce Court in 1857, was only obtainable through a special Act of Parliament, at the impressive sum of £3000 (equivalent to at least 20 times that much in modern terms). The only alternative was for a man to pay the trader's toll and bring his wife to market with a halter around her neck.

One can only hope that these arrangements sometimes brought a genuine improvement to the physical and emotional lives of those concerned.

5th - ITCHING TO REBEL - JACOBITES IN DERBY

Charles Edward Stuart and his Jacobite rebels arrived in Derby on this day in 1745, preceded by a vanguard of 30 men. Hoping for support from the many Catholic sympathisers amongst Derbyshire aristocracy, they crossed their fingers, commandeered horses and demanded billets for more than 9,000 soldiers. The nervous townsfolk rang bells and lit bonfires to welcome the rebels; but the hoped-for support and levies of men were not forthcoming.

The invaders played to the sensibilities of their reluctant hosts as much as they could, and most of their flags displayed St George crosses. Visually, however, they were a little alarming. Reportage singles out the pipers as being shabby and ill-kempt; and there were several old men and young boys in the host too, some shoeless.

Disheartened by the absence of support from his friend Colonel Pole of Radbourne Hall, Bonnie Prince Charlie arrived in the town at dusk to discuss the next step with his men, who were fed well and treated with great respect. The next morning they made themselves less popular, commandeering goods and gear, weapons, clothes and shoes. They had it proclaimed that all people liable for excise taxes should pay up now, under threat of military execution. Adding £100 from the Post Office to the swag, they left two days after their arrival, having mustered just three volunteers from the populace.

In the following year an article appeared in *The Gentlemen's Magazine*, (reprinted in *Nottinghamshire and Derbyshire Notes and Queries*, 1892), written by one of the locals whose house was commandeered for billeting a large chunk of the newly arrived army. The writer emphasises the tattered nature of the troops, and makes some fascinating suggestions as to what the Scots really wore under their kilts:

'...and under their plaids nothing but a various sort of butchering weapons were to be seen: the sight at first must be thought shocking and terrible... My hall (after these vagabond creatures began to be warm, by such numbers under the straw, and a great fire near them) stunk so of their itch, and other nastinesses about them, as if they had been so many persons in a condemn'd hole, and 'twill be very happy if they've left no contagion behind them... To Friday morning they eat me up near a side of beef, 8 joints of mutton, 4 cheeses, with abundance of white and brown bread (particularly white), 3 couple of fowls, and would have drams continually, as well as strong ale, beer, tea, &c. ...I cannot omit taking notice of the generous present they

made me at parting on Friday morning, for the trouble
and expense I was at, and the dangers undergone...
which was a regiment of lice, several loads of their
filthy excrements, and other ejections of different
colours, scatter'd before my door, in the garden,
and elsewhere about my house.'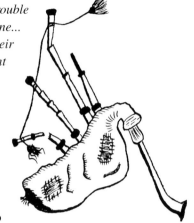

Derby was as far south as the Jacobites
advanced. They had expected certain money
and support from further south in the country,
but it failed to materialise. But it was still to the
amazement of most contemporaries, given their
unimpeded march south, when they chose to head
back up through Ashbourne and across to
Macclesfield and Manchester, prior to their eventual defeat by the King's army under
the Duke of Cumberland. Charles himself had been against the retreat, but he bowed
to the wisdom of his increasingly despondent generals.

9th - MAID IN HEAVEN - ASHFORD

When Ann Swindel of Ashford-in-the-Water died on this day in 1798, her young
friends constructed a Maiden's Garland for her. It can still be seen in Ashford church,
and carries the inscription:

> *Be always ready, no time to delay,*
> *I in my youth was called away.*
> *Great grief to those that's left behind,*
> *But I hope I'm great joy to find.*   (See April 12th)

10th - MELANDRAMATIC - MELANDRA CASTLE

Melandra Castle, near Glossop, was an unknown antiquity until the Rev. John
Watson of Stockport identified it as a Roman fort, and wrote the first ever description
of the site. This was read to the Society of Antiquities in London on December 10th
1772, and archaeological inquiry has continued ever since.

The Castle itself was long gone, and an inscribed stone discovered in a
farmhouse wall nearby spoke of the fate of much of the building material of the old
fort. This stone read, in translation, *'Valerius Vitalis, commanding a company of the*
first Cohort of Frisians, was stationed here.' We tend to think the Germanic
invasions of the post-Roman period were the first occasions on which tribes such as
the Frisians, Jutes, Angles and Saxons occupied the island; but such men were
working in the Roman army 500 years before those later incursions.

Tradition maintains that the building of Melandra Castle came at dear cost to the native British tribe, the Coritani. Somewhere near their own Mouselow Castle is a field formerly known as Almen's Death, where several weapons of war have been unearthed. Here, says folklore, 'All-men' of the Coritani fell at the hands of the Romano-Frisian invaders. The nearby place-name Redgate is said to hark back to the blood shed on the battlefields here.

The one thing that hasn't been entirely nailed down over the years is the origin of the name Melandra. Watson thought it was Greek-derived and that it meant *'the white flowered herb amongst the corn'*. By 1912 archaeologists were suggesting that it came from Molendinarium, meaning 'place of mills'. Melandra Castle - or the suggested Roman form Molendinaria Castra - would therefore mean Mill, or Miller's, Castle.

Alternatively, it could have been a Roman adoption of an older British place name. In Welsh - which is the modern form of the ancient British tongue - melin means 'mill'. Then again, it may be named after melandryum, a Roman word for oak timber. Wood featured heavily in the defences at the Castle, and this derivation would make it Oak Castle, or Wood Castle.

Then again, equally tempting is the notion that it comes from the British/Welsh phrase Moel Andras, meaning the Devil's hill or fort. Such a colourful title might happily have lingered after the departure of the Romans, a folk memory of the powerful foe and conqueror who once had camped there.

However, it may all be far more prosaic than that. The stone used for the main edifice at Melandra was a tawny, yellowish sandstone. In British/Welsh, the word for this tawny colour is melyndra. As ever in folklore, truth is often duller than fiction.

12th - LOVE FALLS ON STONEY GROUND - STONEY MIDDLETON

Dwelling morbidly on her fickle lover William Barnsley, the jilted Hannah Baddeley decided to end it all by jumping over a cliff at Stoney Middleton. Luckily, her voluminous underwear came to the rescue and the petticoats acted as a crude parachute. Scratched, shaken and stirred, Hannah nevertheless survived, and she was escorted home by alarmed villagers. The site of the failed suicide has since been known as Lover's Leap. It appears that her cuts and bruises were more than skin-deep, however, for the poor girl died two years later at the age of 26, on this day in 1764.

This is one of many such Leaps in the country, and there are others in Derbyshire itself - near Sharplow Point in Dovedale; and at a narrow point in Ashwood Dale, Buxton. In the latter the name was bestowed after an eloping couple leaped across to freedom on a horse. (See March 25th).

Folklore has played a large part in fleshing out the legends; but Hannah Baddeley's tale is generally accepted as true. Richard Keane, in his *A Six Days' Ramble Over Derbyshire Hills and Dales, in the Year 1858*, notes of his visit to Stoney Middleton: *'Here we found William Wood, the historian of Eyam, who had been waiting for us some time at the 'Lover's Leap' Inn. We took two views here* [i.e. Keane was a photographer], *showing the fine rock, which Mr. Wood assures is a genuine Lover's Leap; that a young woman of the name of Baddaley, about a hundred years ago, threw herself in a fit of disappointed love from this height, and miraculously escaped with her life, her petticoat forming a parachute, and her fall being further broken by the boughs of a small yew-tree growing in the crevices of the rock; she fell into a saw-pit, and, though bruised and disfigured, was able to limp home, where she lived many years in a state of single blessedness.'*

The happy ending in this version is the only dodgy detail.

13th - VICAR LOCKS YOUNG LOVERS IN CHURCH - RICHARD FURNESS OF EYAM

Born in Eyam in 1791, Richard Furness achieved fame in the 19th century as a poet and much else besides. In his teens he turned from working the family farm to become an apprentice in the relatively lucrative trade of weaving in Chesterfield. He also became involved with the Methodist church, and before his teens were out he was a part-time hellfire preacher.

Never one to stay still for too long, Furness did a stint in the volunteer army in London (this being the tail-end of the Napoleonic Wars); and in 1816 he eloped with Frances Ibbotson of Hathersage, persuading the Vicar there to lock them in the sanctuary of the church until 8am the following morning, when they could be legally married. Frances' father, a Catholic, soon accepted the rogue Methodist as a valid son-in-law.

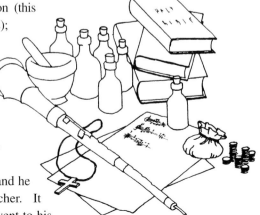

Married life was kind to Furness, and he took a position at Dore as school-teacher. It was during this time that he gave full vent to his poetical skills, earning himself the title 'The Parnassus of the Peak' (William Newton having snatched the 'Minstrel of the Peak' tag some decades earlier). The title is a reference to the mountain in central Greece, home to Apollo and the Muses, synonymous with poetical genius.

Richard died on December 13th 1857, and folk from Eyam carried the body back home over the moor by candlelight to show their respect. The Parnassus was duly buried in Eyam churchyard. Although he penned a *'Farewell, vain world...'* epitaph for himself, the best postscript comes from an earlier work by the man, describing his various skills and roles in Dore:

> *I, Richard Furness, schoolmaster, Dore,*
> *Keep parish books and pay the poor;*
> *Draw plans for buildings and indite*
> *Letters for those who cannot write;*
> *Make wills and recommend proctor,*
> *Cure wounds, let blood with any doctor;*
> *Draw teeth, sing psalms, the hautboy play* [NB a kind of oboe]
> *At chapel on each holy day;*
> *Paint sign-boards, cut names at command,*
> *Survey and plot estates of land,*
> *Collect at Easter, one in ten* [NB the church tithe]
> *And on Sunday, say Amen.*

20th - SWEARING CONSTABLES - BAKEWELL

Like any other workers facing the redundancies threatened by technological innovation, farm workers have never taken kindly to the introduction of labour-saving machinery. Journal keeper White Watson of Bakewell, writing in the 1830s, gives an insight into the riots that resulted from the early steps of agricultural mechanisation. Expecting mounting problems nationally, the policy was to bolster every region by 'swearing in' new police:

'December 1830. There being tribes of incendiaries in various parts of the kingdom, burning corn stacks, threshing machines, buildings, etc., to a very great amount; it is thought right for the magistrates in every town and village throughout the kingdom to obtain lists of all the householders, and to swear in special constables. December 20th and 21st swearing in days at Bakewell.'

21st - St Thomas the Apostle's Day - TAKING ALMS - NO DOUBT ABOUT IT

St Thomas the Apostle's Day is the foremost day in the year for handing out alms, and, not surprisingly, for seeking them. In many parts of Derbyshire and the Peak poor folk would beg wheat from their neighbours today, for the purpose of baking the traditional Christmas morning breakfast of frummity (wheat slow-cooked in milk - a cross between porridge and Christmas pudding).

Do-gooders would often stipulate this day in their wills for token generosity. Take the unfortunate Thomas Smith, for example: *'Thomas Smith of Kimberley left by a will bearing date 1767 - 20£ to the poor of the Parish of Smalley the interest of which was to be distributed to them in bread on S. Thomas' Day... It is understood that the said Thomas Smith was killed by the fall of a tree.'* (from the Registers of Morley and Smalley)

In 1439, one John Herresoun arranged for alms to be delivered to himself on this day, according to a record in the Glapwell Charters. He handed over all his lands to one John Halton and his wife, on condition that they should provide him for the rest of his life with daily estovers - that is, all life's daily essentials in food, drink, clothing, footwear, linen, sheets, etc. When Herresoun died the Haltons were to provide a cow worth seven shillings to pay for his funeral and tomb. The indenture is dated *21st December - in festo sancti Thome apostoli - 1439.*

For more on the Glapwell Charters see June 11th.

24th - FISHY BOGGARTS - BRADWELL, CHAPEL-EN-LE-FRITH

The malevolent Derbyshire spirits known as boggarts are an odd mixture of fairy and poltergeist. The most famous one was the Lumb Boggart which began haunting Bradwell following the discovery of a woman's bones beneath a staircase there in 1760. Bringing misfortune and broken crockery, the Boggart escalated its violent haunting until villagers were forced to summon an exorcist, at which point things became even more surreal. Struggling with the entity, the exorcist cried out *'Beroald, beroald, gab gabor agaba!'*, which forced the spirit to manifest itself. Seizing the initiative the exorcist then transformed it into a small fish, commanding it to live at Lumb Mouth, the source of Bradwell Beck.

As a bizarre consolation the Boggart was allowed to transform itself into a white ouzel every Christmas Eve and fly two miles to Lumbley Pool between Bamford and Brough.

Dr Clegg, Physician and diary-keeper of Chapel-en-le-Frith, came across a particularly pestilential boggart. Writing in 1730 of a smallpox outbreak, he says that a stricken boy and his parents, sharing a bed, *'heard a noise as if someone had walked sharply over the chamber and gone under the bed. The husband got up and searched the room, but found nothing. The child lay betwixt them... but presently cried out, 'Ye Boggart has touched me'... A night or two before ye wife, being in ye house herself, heard a dismall noise like ye cry of a child, ending in a mournful tone. Ye like walking she heard again in ye chamber ye week but one after, when her sister's child was seized with the most violent and deadly infection I have ever seen.'*

Much of the boggart tradition can be put down to parents using the spirit as a bogey-man. When children were naughty or needed to heed a warning they were told *'The Boggart'll tak thee...'*

CHRISTMAS CUSTOMS

24th - ROAR HIDE - BRADWELL

Boggarts apart, the 24th was Bradwell's Mischief Night, when boys engaged in the very dubious tradition of Bull Roaring. This involved stuffing drainpipes with newspaper and setting them alight, and then running for cover. The noise, apparently, was a dead ringer for the bellowing of an angry bull. As was the irate cry of the householder, no doubt.

In the same village, and in neighbouring lead-mining communities, the men would seek out a particularly impressive lump of lead ore at this time of year. The humble treasure was decorated with greenery and candles, and old carols were sung around it. Candles were left in the mine workings on Christmas Eve too, for a character called The Old Man, representing the spirit of all the miners who had gone before.

24th - HOT POT SHOT - ASHFORD IN THE WATER

In *Customs and Notions at Ashford-In-The-Water Sixty Years Ago*, an article penned by Thomas Brushfield JP and printed in the July 1884 *Reliquary*, we gain an insight into the near-universal rural Christmas tradition of posset-drinking:

'Another custom I believe is yet partially observed. On Christmas Eve it was very common to have posset for supper, when little parties met to partake of the meal, and a vessel, made specially for the purpose and the occasion, called a posset-pot, found a place on the pantry shelves in every house in the village. A small silver coin and a ring were put into the posset, and the persons who partook of it, numbering half a dozen, sometimes more, took each in turn a spoonful. If one of the young party fished up the coin with the

POSSET POT

spoon, such person was considered certain of good luck during the coming year, and an early and a happy marriage was considered equally certain to fall to the lot of the one who had the good fortune to fish up the ring.'

The posset pots themselves were usually two-handled cups, about seven inches high and decorated with flowers. They often had personal inscriptions. The posset itself consisted of sweetened hot milk and ale, spiced with nutmeg.

25th - CHRISTMAS FOLK TRADITIONS - CAROLS IN DISGUISE

Carol-singing has lingered in some North Derbyshire and South Yorkshire villages as a pub tradition of communal singing. Not just a drunken chorus of *O Come all ye Faithful* and an afternoon of shopping precinct muzak, but a collection of unique, low-church-flavoured 17th and 18th century variants on old favourites and obscure pieces alike.

Some are even older - the carol *Down In Yon Forest* is a truly ancient folk song. It belongs, strictly speaking, to Corpus Christi Day (the Thursday following the 8th Sunday after Easter), and its plot concerning Jesus as a wounded and bleeding night in a castle in the middle of a forest is very weird, and very haunting. Seek it out, and you'll soon be joining the Campaign For Real Carols.

This is one tradition where church and pub have taken an equal hand in the development of the style. The familiar door-to-door farrago owes more of its history to wassailing customs (see December 26th). The Peak District carols do a lot of 'fugueing' - repeating certain lines with lots of glorious harmonies.

Some of the best survivals can be savoured over a couple of swift ones in Castleton, Hathersage, Stannington, Dungworth, Ecclesfield and other locations - keep your eye on the local press for wheres and whens. Get your hands on some of the recorded versions beforehand, to get a head start on the unique melody lines. The songs are magnificent, the atmosphere is wonderful, and you'll never want to sing *While Shepherds Watched* to the dull familiar tune again.

Other Christmas folk traditions like to serve their music with a little horse play. Guisering is an old term for fancy dress, and it involved some accompanying music, ritual and begging. Derby Tup, or Derby Ram, guisering was still thriving at Christmastime before the First World War. In Castleton the guisers would dress as each of the key characters in their song - a boy in a sack to represent the sheep, often with a real sheep's head on top, sometimes a model one; one as a butcher carrying a knife; one dressed as a woman; and one carrying a bowl. Their song commenced:

'As I was going to Derby upon a market day, I met the finest Tupsie that ever was fed on hay'. Two of the characters are later described: *'The man that stuck the tupsie was up to the knees in blood; The man that held the basin was washed away in the flood'.* As the song described the diverse fates of the giant beast's ears, eyes, skin, horns, etc., the guisers used to act out the scene and then beg for money.

An alternative form of guisering was the Old Horse. This was common in the north of the county, recorded in places such as Norton, Eckington and Dronfield. At Eyam and Little Hucklow the horse was called Ball. Boisterous men did the aggressive rounds of the houses, the horse usually being a sheet of tarpaulin topped with a wooden horse head, complete with snapping jaws. At some locations, including Eckington, they often went to the grave of a dead horse for a real head, putting bottle bottoms in the eye sockets for added effect. At Eyam the horse skull was lit eerily from the inside with a candle. The Old Horse party's door-to-door song was:

OLD 'TUP'
CASTLETON
1910

It is a poor old horse, and he's knocking at your door
And if you'll please to let him in he'll please you all,
I'm sure Poor old horse, poor old horse!

The song then describes the horse's decay from young, well tended and fed, to old, decrepit and uncared for:

He once was a young horse and in his youthful prime,
my master used to ride on him and thought him very fine;
And now that he's grown old and nature doth decay,
My master frowns upon him and these words I've heard him say -
Poor old horse, poor old horse!

So take him and whip him, to the huntsman he shall go,
To his tender carcase the hounds will not say no -
Poor old horse, poor old horse!

After several other verses and some knockabout prose, the horse is given a new lease of life, magically reborn. The whole thing brings luck and renewed prosperity to householders at the end of the year.

These traditions have all the hallmarks of something truly ancient. Then again, so does the Ploughman's Lunch, and that was just a marketing ploy in the 1960s. We will never know for certain the origins of such arcane practices as the Old Horse and Derby Tup; but it is somehow reassuring that the famous sheep, at least, is not quite dead.

The Derby Ram song is still widely sung, his face leers from the Derby County football club badge, and the guiser characters - the shepherd, his wife, the butcher, the butcher boys and the Tup himself - crop up regularly in local carnivals and parades.

25th - CHRISTMAS HOLLY - A BURNING QUESTION - EYAM

It is unlucky to burn holly which has been used for Christmas decoration. A tale from Eyam describes how, in the cottage where the plague first broke out, a man was burning holly after Christmas, as a direct result of which his chimney caught fire. In attempting to contain the blaze the man chopped down an adjoining wooden flue (used for drawing off steam from the copper over the fire), and found a heavy bundle concealed inside.

Whatever it was, it was probably hidden there at the time of the plague. The man told his neighbours he had burnt the bundle for fear of infection; but, as Richard Keene wrote in his 1858 *Ramble Over Derbyshire Hills and Dales*, having taken the story from an old Eyam resident, *'he soon after left the house and appeared in much better circumstances. Thus, instead of ill-luck, the burning of the holly proved a very fortunate event for him.'*

25th - WAKING UP WITH SAW-HEADS - TIDESWELL, HADDON HALL

Formerly when pigs were killed for a Christmas feast, the fry was given to a needy neighbour. The plate upon which the gory gift was presented was not to be washed, however. Local lore maintained: *'If you wash the plate upon which the fry is brought to you, the pig won't take salt.'*

The housekeeping records of Haddon Hall for Christmas 1663 offer a cosy insight into the festivities and kitchen chores for that year. The biggest pay-packet went to the tireless cook George Wood. He received £3 for his two-week Christmas stint, with another £1 and five shillings for his assistant. Three shillings for general kitchen and table duties over the festive season were given to Anthony Higton, officially titled 'Turnspit'. Widow Creswick was given three-and-six *'for pulling Fowls and pulling all Christmas'*; and three shillings went to Catherine Sprig for helping the scullery maid.

The splendidly named entertainer Ottiwel Bromwell was given 10 shillings for dancing, and another five shillings were handed out to *'Ottiwel Bromwell's Kinswoman'* for the same service. Thomas Shaw, the piper, and his band provided the accompanying music - the records tell us that Shaw received £2 *'for pipering all Christmas'*, while the rest of the band shared 10 shillings between them. Shaw was clearly the star of the show.

Originally established as a basic insurance protection plan in the event of bovine disease or death, the Tideswell and Litton United Cow Club still meets for a private function at Christmas, the Cow Club Dinner. The Club was founded on March 25th 1838 to ensure that an ill cow did not bring economic disaster to its owner. A member has access to free veterinary treatment, and the full value of the beast if it dies, with the conditions: *'no more than £14, and the hide, carcase and tallow belong to the club.'* The sums involved have not altered with the passing of the years - needless to say, membership these days is for the sake of tradition rather than financial security.

The establishment of the Club should have buried forever the traditional

Derbyshire slander which insists that all Tideswell people are soft in the head. Known as 'Tidsa Sawyeds', they were said to have gained the name after sawing off the head of a cow trapped in a barred gate, a rescue bid doomed to failure.

25th - CHRISTMAS ALL MONTH LONG

The old concept of Advent has now become a month-long Christmas extravaganza, and not many places in the county escape the ravages of Santa, seasonal muzak and plastic fir trees. There are several popular seasonal events for children throughout the county and National Park. Highlights include brass band-accompanied carol singing in Peak Cavern, Castleton; and the arrival of Father Christmas in the candlelit splendour of Poole's Cavern in Buxton. Santa spreads himself thinly, as ever, and in addition to the many Grottoes he also hitches a lift on a steam train at Matlock.

Towns and villages vie to out-Yule each other; but the Christmas lights of Great Hucklow are famous, and rightly so, while the Dickens-flavoured Christmas markets and merriment of Buxton, Ashbourne and Bakewell should momentarily prevent you muttering 'humbug'.

26th - HUTCHINSON TAKES AN EARLY BATH - MATLOCK

Not the most ancient of traditions, but the Matlock Raft Race is a firm fixture in the Christmas calendar in these parts. It takes place along the Derwent, a 3 km stretch from Matlock Bridge to Cromford Bridge. Fancy dress is the order of the day, and many of the rafts are suitable monstrosities. The event is arranged by the Matlock branch of the Sub Aqua Club for members and guests, and although entry is free a donation to charity is encouraged. Highlights of the watery course include the three-foot high weir at Cromford Mill. The event kicks off soon after 10.00am.

Matlock's fame these days is based largely on the tourist-lure of Matlock Bath. The town has always had its advocates, however, even if no writer in recent times has quite managed to summon the passion of Chapel-en-le-Frith writer John Hutchinson in 1810, writing in his peon to purple prose, *The Romantic Beauties of Matlock:*

Matlock is yet unhonoured and, almost, undescribed... If a general description of this sequestered dale were to be attempted, it might be compared with the imaginary Elysium of the ancients... The neat white cottages of the different inhabitants, perched on the solid foundation of the majestic rock that rises perpendicular, or o'erhangs its base, are productive of the most novel sensations. The axial inhabitants seem as if they were in the first stage of a transmutation from grovelling man, and gradually abstracting the mind from all earthly considerations, to be ascending, in thought, towards that divine source, from whence all beauty and loveliness are derived.

28th - TIME TAKES ITS TOLL AT SWARKESTON

Swarkeston bridge crosses the Trent near Stanton. It was one of the longest bridges in the country when first built in the 13th century (possibly as early as 1192). Legend says that it was erected by two sisters who lost their lovers as they attempted to return across the storm-swollen Trent. The forlorn women spent all their money erecting the bridge and never married, living the rest of their days in poverty and mourning. The bridge is nearly three quarters of a mile long.

At the bridge's centre there was an ancient chapel in which a priest - living, in effect, as a hermit - was paid to sing mass regularly. The man was supplied by the Priory of Repton, who had been given some meadow land between the bridge and Ingleby to pay for the office. The hermit priest's job description said he must pray for the King, the benefactors of the bridge, and the God-speed of all travellers.

He was also responsible for a lantern to light the way across at night. Most representations of St Christopher carrying Christ across the river depict a man on the bank wielding a lantern - this seems to be the image which inspired the office of the bridge priest-cum-hermit. The chapel at Swarkeston was reported as standing as late as 1863, although by then it had been relocated to a meadow on the riverbank.

By the 14th century the bridge was ruinous enough for Edward III, on December 28th 1347, to grant two Swarkeston nobles the right to collect tolls for three years, for the sole purpose of raising money to repair the bridge. Crossing with cartloads of hay, hides, fleeces, fish, salt, ale, charcoal, etc. cost a farthing, as did *'any horse, mare, ox or cow'*. More expensive items included wine casks and metals, at 2d; goatskin leather and cartloads of cloth, at 3d; and, most expensive of all, boxes of Allecis, at 6d. These were small fish, salted like anchovies.

In 1503 an inquest heard that there had been no priest appointed to the chapel for 20 years. The furniture, even the glass and iron bars of the windows, had been removed by one Mr Edward Beamont of Arleston, *'and we say that if the Chapel decay, the bridge will not stand'*, warned the accusers.

There have been many repairs over the years. The modern bridge was rebuilt in 1801, and again later in the century, although some of the original structure can still be discerned.

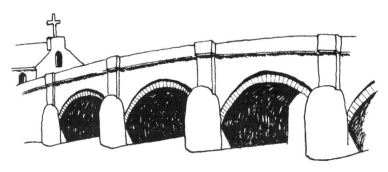

INDEX